UNSTUCK

An Audacious Hunt for
Home and Happiness

RACHAEL HERRON

ISBN: 978-1-940785-70-7

HGA Publishing

Contents

For Lala. Wherever we are is where I want to be.

Chapter 1

The Impossible Idea is Floated

One night in October, our neighbor Megan comes over and falls into our couch. What happens next is really all her fault.

It's 2020, smack-bang mid-pandemic, and she's the only podmate my wife Lala and I have. When Megan visits, we smother her with love not just because she's lovable, but because she's someone *different* to talk to.

On this night, Megan sits next to our old dog, Clementine, who gives her the pit bull lean of love. The ancient boy-kittens fight to perch on her thighs. Even Dozy, the youngest animal of the lot, only barks at her for a few seconds before trying to wriggle into her lap.

With a wobbly smile, Megan says, "I might never leave. Or I might take one of these with me." She tries to tuck Dozy under her pajama top. "At least you and Lala have each other. All I have are the stupid pigeons trying to nest in my roof. They smell disgusting and they never even *try* to cuddle me."

I tilt my head, assessing her blue, sushi-covered pajamas. "Are those new? I don't think I've seen those ones before."

"They are!" She looks pleased that I've noticed. "I love my jim-jams."

I realize something. "You know, since you moved here right before lockdown, I don't think I've ever seen you in street clothes. Have I?"

Megan tugs on the hem of her shirt. "What do you mean? I go out in the streets. These *are* my street clothes. And you'd be *shocked* at how well I clean up when I want to. Imagine all this glory—" she wiggles her fingers toward her cheeks "—with makeup. Add a sparkly crop top and jeans? Majestic as hell. Now keep imagining it, 'cause you'll probably never get to see it. At least I'll never have to wear hard pants again."

"I haven't worn jeans once since this started," I say. "Swear to god, I'll never wear a pair that cuts into my waist again. Ever."

She sits up straighter. "Oh! Did you see what your mother country did?"

I have dual citizenship: New Zealand on my mother's side, the US on my father's, but I've only ever visited New Zealand, never lived there. "I don't think so."

She says, "New Zealand went to level one."

I say, "Honestly, I haven't been following them that closely. Is that good or bad?"

"It means they're completely open. Like, no restrictions except you have to wear a mask on public transportation. But nowhere else. Because *they got rid of Covid.*"

Lala and I both sigh deeply.

"Can you imagine?" says Megan. "Those folks down there are just walking around in stores, in restaurants.

Hanging out with their families. Everyone going to work like normal. No masks. No fear. They have five million people, but only twenty-five deaths total."

My chest gets that too-hot feeling. "Yeah. I *can* imagine. If we'd done it right, the US could be like that too, but I read we just passed two hundred and thirty thousand deaths."

Megan slides farther into the couch. "I'd tell you to move there, but then I'd die of loneliness so I won't say that. Oakland needs you. *I* need you."

Lala shrugs. "Eh, we're not going anywhere."

"Maybe someday," I say.

Megan's scowl deepens. "Seriously, though. Why don't you? You're a citizen, right?"

I shake my head. "I wish it were that easy."

"What, is it hard to get a visa for Lala?"

I haven't checked into it for a while, but the last time I did, it appeared to be a matter of paying some money and providing proof that we're legally partnered. I say, "Um, I don't think so."

Megan boggles at us. "What the fuck are you waiting for? You have the *literal* golden ticket! You own one of the top five passports in the whole world! And right now, because of their Covid protocols, they're saying it's jumped to number one."

I give my normal answer. "I know, but my sisters are here. So's our nephew. Our dads are here. Then there's the house and the animals. It's a fun pipe dream sometimes, that's all."

She gestures wildly in the air, and Waylon careens off her lap. "You can see them on Zoom, just like you do now. And they'd visit you. *I* will come visit you, if the world ever reopens. The animals can go with you. You can get out of this backward country, and you're not even *thinking* about it?"

Lala gives Clementine's ear a stroke. "You can't import bully breeds to New Zealand," she says.

There it is. The biggest reason we can't go. We can't go without our old lady pit bull, the sweetest dog that ever dogged, and we would never rehome this huge part of our hearts. It's not even worth talking about.

I ignore the stuck, clogged feeling at the back of my throat.

Giving herself a little shake, Megan says, "Never mind. I hate this idea. Wait, can you adopt me as an adult child? Take me with you? Okay, probably not. So you're not going. You can't go. I'm not losing my only podmates. Forget I said anything."

But I don't forget she said it. It keeps ringing in my ears. *You have the literal golden ticket.*

Later that week, Lala and I eat dinner together as we always do nowadays. It used to be a treat to eat together. Now it feels like the law. Luckily, even after being together for almost seventeen years, I still feel myself light up when I see her, when she gives me that special *aw-shucks* smile that I've never seen her give anyone else. We work well as a team too. I'm a stress-bunny, while she's made of chill. I'll make sure the bills get paid, while she makes sure we're not all work and no play. Lala reminds me to breathe. Sometimes literally. She believes it's going to be okay, and she's usually right. It doesn't hurt that she looks sexier in a flannel shirt and Doc Martens than anyone else in the world.

Tonight, I've made chipotle-honey chicken tacos with

extra avocados and a fresh pickled onion slaw, and I'm happy to be living the soft-pants life.

I rest my forearms on our table, which is made of heavy, dark wood. It's more scuffed than not, a freebie from our realtor who found it abandoned in a house she sold. It's been good to us, holding fifteen years' worth of meals, dinner parties, and cats that we shoo off. It's where we play Azul and talk about how cute our pets are and argue about whose turn it is to do the dishes. It's also a place where important conversations take place.

"Golden ticket," I say.

"I *know*." In the humidity, Lala's curls are as tight as if she'd wound them around pencils. "What are you thinking?"

"I don't know what I'm thinking. I'm confused. Do we want to be here when we're old?"

We are firmly middle-aged right now. I'm forty-eight, and Lala's fifty-two. We're still healthy and strong. I personally think we're fucking *cool* middle-aged people. I'm in a yacht-rock band. Lala is an artist and plays the banjo and seldom has the same hair color for more than a few months. But I know we're not as young as my soul feels.

She says, "You mean do we want to still be in this house when we're old?"

I nod. We live in East Oakland, on a mellow street in one of the toughest parts of the city. We love our friendly cul-de-sac and the creek that winds behind the house and the sound of football games at the high school on the other side of the creek. But it's still rough. To walk our dogs, we have to adhere to our zigzagged mental map of the few blocks that don't routinely have aggressive dogs on the loose. Speaking of walking, there is nothing to walk *to*. Literally nothing. Not a cafe, not a single grocery store or bank. Even the only corner liquor store closed recently. We hear gunshots every single night. A man was murdered directly across the street. I've held ice to a young man's head who was pistol-whipped and thrown out of a speeding car right in front of our door. Even knowing the high rate of crime, I'd always felt safe here until I installed the Citizen app on my phone a few months back. Citizen alerted me whenever there was crime nearby. Like, it *sent me a push notification,* so I learned that all the thumps and bumps and shouts I heard were actually really bad, shitty things happening all around me. It was a screwed-up thing to subject my adrenal system to, and three days after I installed the app, I deleted it, preferring to ostrich my head in the sand. But I admit I'm still shaken.

We've talked at length about moving to a cheaper part of the country, but unfortunately, cheaper parts of the United States also tend to be more closed-minded toward gay people. By living in the San Francisco Bay Area for so long, we've gotten used to living in a place filled with people who think we have the right to exist.

It's a trap—one that we're privileged enough to call our own—but a trap nonetheless. We bought our house with money we didn't have just before the 2008 recession (partially caused by people buying houses with money they didn't have, whoops!). Almost immediately, our house was worth a quarter of what we'd mortgaged it for. For fifteen years, we've been making the mortgage payments, but we've only just turned right side up, equity-wise. If we sell this house and remove the small amount of equity we've built up, we won't ever be able to afford to live in the Bay Area again. If we leave, we can't come back.

In spite of that scary thought, I say, "It's hard enough to

navigate the neighborhood now. What about in thirty years? Are we going to feel safe on the bus when we can't drive?"

"Probably not. And you can't get the medical care you need right now. How much harder is that going to get?"

I had recently struggled with a mystery illness that kept me in intense pain for about three months. During those months our insurance company denied me, in this order: antibiotics, pain medicine, two ultrasounds, one CT scan, two MRIs, and a colonoscopy. We racked up dozens of hours on the phone, fighting every denial, before I finally got what I needed (a simple diagnosis of diverticulitis that could have been treated so much earlier). And we know we're the lucky ones. We had the time and energy and money to fight the system. We've both been bubbling at a constant raging boil because of it, furious that *this* is what the country we live in has become: a place ruled by the almighty dollar wielded by lobbyists, not by simple, decent human rights.

I say, "New Zealand has socialized medicine." I bite the inside of my mouth where it's raw from me worrying at it. "Do you honestly see this country going to single-payer healthcare anytime soon?"

She shakes her head. "No. So what? Are we actually thinking about this? Moving to New Zealand?"

"I mean, *are* we?" I look down at the orange dog with the silver muzzle at my feet. "But Clementine. We can't leave her behind."

Lala says, "What's that visa I would need?"

I looked it up just this afternoon. "A Partner of a New Zealander Work Visa."

"How long did you say it takes to get?"

"People on Reddit said about a year."

"And if I got it, how long would we have to enter the country?"

This answer I knew for sure, because I'd called New Zealand Immigration to ask. "Twelve months after they grant the application."

"So if we apply for my visa, we'd have about two years to get ready to move."

I nod and look again at Clementine. She's battling kidney disease and pancreatitis. She's already enrolled in pet hospice, although she's done so well, she's actually come *off* hospice a couple of times. She's on multiple medicines to keep her happy and comfortable. She won't last two years, but I'm not going to be the one to say it.

I do say, "What about the others? The cats are old too." Waylon and Willie might live another few years, but the internet tells us they're too old to safely make the journey and quarantine.

Lala says, "How about we cross that bridge if we get to it?"

Neither of us makes a dark joke about the rainbow bridge, and for this we deserve several medals.

I nod toward our five-year-old Maltipoo, the one I found stray in front of our house one day. "Okay, then, what about Dozy? She's young enough, right? To make it through the quarantine? But... it costs seven to ten thousand dollars to import a dog."

"Jesus!"

"We'd have to add it to the budget and save for it. Speaking of that, how much do you think it costs to move to another country?"

"It has to cost a *lot*."

No, we can't do this. This life is what we've chosen.

This mortgage. These bills. It's fine. It'll have to continue to be fine.

But then, in a sudden verbal move I don't see coming, Lala says, "Let's just do it."

A jolt thuds through my torso. "Do *what*?"

"Go. Move."

My fingers dig into my thighs. I take a beat to breathe. Then another. "Move?"

"Move," she says again.

I can't leave this home. This house is the only place I've ever lived with Lala. When we moved in, it felt like we were kids. We grew up here. Fifteen years' worth of love are in these walls. Leaving this home? By choice? Who would do that?

I feel so stuck.

But feeling stuck is normal. It's part of being an adult. Right?

And anyway, if I feel trapped right now, it's only because I've shackled myself to what I wanted. Or at least, what I thought I wanted. A mortgage so big it feels like we'll never pay it off. No good retirement plan. Fear about aging and changes in health.

Stuck.

It comes out of my mouth in a surprise bellow. "Okay, let's go!"

We grin at each other.

"Really?" I say.

"Why not?" she says.

Seriously? We could do this? Are we *allowed*? To just up and move to New Zealand?

It is, after all, the land of my mother, of my forebears. I come from hardy sheep farming stock—those antipodean pastures are in my blood, aren't they?

Yes, I can see it! We'll be brave! We'll be explorers! Adventurers! Maybe we'll take up some hearty sport that makes our blood pump harder—white water rafting or long-distance hiking.

We're *moving*! Our grins expand. My heart thumps, equal parts excited and terrified.

Then a migraine fells me almost instantly, the blood pumping too hard through my body.

I'm going to have to work on this if I want to be a sporty Kiwi.

Chapter 2

Impossible Questions With Ridiculous Answers

Here's the thing—neither of us has any idea how to move to another country. It's *so exciting*. It's also impossible to get our heads around.

I make a brain dump list that includes:

Sell the house

Get rid of almost everything we own

Leave the US, enter NZ

Figure out how to start to do even one of these things

This is too hard already.

"So how about this?" I call out from the bedroom where I'm lying flat, staring at the ceiling. Lala hates it when I yell across the house, but this is important. "We could *not* move."

She stomps out of her office and leans in the doorway. "That would be easier, yes. You want to do that?"

I want to...

I want to come unstuck.

"No. I want to move."

A grunt, and I'm alone again with the ceiling. Was that

crack always there? Will that make it harder to sell the house?

We're not there yet, thank god. All we need to do right now is the smallest, tiniest thing. We send in an application for a Partner of a New Zealander Work Visa for Lala. It only takes about ten (hair-raising) minutes to fill out.

Then we decide to make no other decisions until Clementine is no longer with us. That decision is a good one, but it also feels deeply fucked-up to be planning something around the death of a beloved member of our family.

Our dinner table conversations change.

I ask, "Where would you want to live in New Zealand?"

We glance furtively at Clementine, who stands next to the table hoping for the thousandth time that she is a sushi dog. Admittedly, sometimes she *is* a sushi dog, an ecstatic one, but tonight we're having steak cooked in butter. Rudely, her pancreas won't allow her to be a buttered-steak dog.

I correct myself. "I mean, if we go, are we still thinking about Wellington?"

We're back to saying *if* we go, even though we know we're moving. We've decided, and while Lala and I tend to adult on the college dorm level (see the battered couch that still smells like our border collie, Clara, who died last year), we're pretty good at making big, hard decisions and following through on them.

We just can't say that it's a for-sure in front of Clemmy, who's still insisting with the power of her mind that she *can* eat fatty steak, no problem, nosirree.

Then, one day, a few months later, our darling dies.

That makes it sound easy, as if Clementine went peacefully in her sleep with no assistance from us. She did not. Our stupid animals never do. We keep them healthy and strong, so that every single damn time, *we* have to decide that today is the day we should allow them to leave their bodies. Her hospice nurse comes, and Clementine goes to sleep in our arms. It's unbearable.

We both cry ourselves to sleep.

The very next day, Lala's visa arrives in my inbox.

But—we only applied for it three months ago! Wasn't it supposed to take a year? I read and reread the email, sure that it can't possibly be the real thing. This is her *visa*? The thing that will let her into a country that isn't letting in anyone but citizens, their partners, and essential medical personnel?

I dash into Lala's office. "Look. It came. Your visa. It *came*. Can you read it? Is this actually it?"

She looks at my phone. "Holy shit. But it says we have six months to enter."

That's why I can't believe it's a real visa. "Remember, I called them to double-check? The immigration person said the entrance time after you get the visa is twelve months. And she worked there, so she would know, right?"

Lala's eyes are so wide I can see the whites encircling her pupils. "Can we call them again?"

So we do. The counselor looks up Lala's application and says, "Six months is correct. You must enter the country before the nineteenth of August. But the managed isolation quarantine hotels are booking up months in advance, so you'd do well to get in earlier, if you can manage it."

There's no extension available.

It's February. We'd kind of been thinking we'd move to New Zealand in eighteen months or so. Now, we need to leave in fewer than six.

A knot of anxiety forms in my stomach, taking up residence, apparently. I can almost hear it putting up shelves and moving furniture around. Sure, my *anxiety's* got a comfy new place to live. Me, I've got to start dismantling my home.

I've felt trapped. But I'm not sure where to find the bravery to start.

I do love a deadline, though.

So we're doing it, even if that means we're doing it scared.

I notify the anxiety in my stomach that if it wants a safe corner to live in, it should move a little to the left. Excitement wants to renovate too, and it's got a big hammer to swing.

Then I wonder if I'll ever love another dining table as much as I do the creaky one we sit at every night.

One morning, over yogurt and granola, I ask, "When are you going to tell HR?"

Lala thinks she can probably keep her web developer job while in New Zealand, but she's not *totally* sure. "Soon. I guess. Yeah, soon."

"Okay." I pause before I pluck my next worry out of the air. "What if when we get there, no one likes us?"

She talks around a mouthful of banana. "Eh. We're quite likable. And by we, I mean you. I'm an ogre, obviously."

"Obviously. Seriously, though, what are you most nervous about?"

"What do you mean?"

"Tell me your biggest fear. The one that would keep you awake at night if you weren't such a good sleeper." At the moment, I don't have just one top worry. I have three: that we'll regret moving so far away from our loved ones, that some unforeseen challenge will break our hearts, and that we won't be able to afford life in a new country. But I'm tired of listening to my brain freak out. I want to listen to Lala. To help her, if I can.

"All right," she says. "Don't laugh."

I cross my heart and shake my head. "Of course I won't."

"I'm really worried about being cold."

It's a miracle that I do not laugh, but that's marriage, littered with unforeseen challenges that we must rise to or pay the emotional toll. "Okay," I say. "Yes. All right."

This is the fault of the New Zealand home improvement show we've been watching. A house they restored had no insulation at all. As in, they ripped out the drywall, and the beams behind it were naked and shivering. This sent Lala down a research rabbit hole, and it turns out this is normal. Apparently, Kiwis, as a nation, have been very cavalier about insulating houses. Even though New Zealand gets quite cold in winter, *ninety-five percent of homes* don't have central heat. Instead, people use heat pumps and electric heaters, and a whopping thirty-four percent of homes use wood fires as their main source of heating.

This explains so much about the house where I lived during high school and undergrad, the house where my dad still lives, which has no heat except for the living room fireplace. Yes, it's California, but it freezes in the winter, and that house got *cold*. My Kiwi mom, though, didn't want to pay for central heating installation. The fireplace was good enough for her. If we weren't in the living room, we just bundled up. I spent a lot of time reading under the covers by flashlight. And even now, I like a bit of a draft. When I sleep, I like the room to be as cold as humanly possible, and I still keep the fan directed right at me, year-round. Obnoxiously, I'm of the belief that being cold is empirically better than being hot. After all, you can always put on a sweater. You can always do some jumping jacks to move the blood if you've been sitting a while. You can always put on some wool socks that your wife made you, out of your vast collection of *many* wife-knitted wool socks.

I give Lala a Band-Aid offering. "I'll make you another sweater."

She shakes her head. "You don't understand how miserable being cold can be. My mom used to find me asleep on top of the heat register in the bathroom when I was a kid. I *hate* being cold."

"Being cold is nice!" Because directly contradicting your partner always goes well.

"Being warm is nicer!"

Virtuously, I say, "I actually *like* feeling cold. Temperature control. Having cold feet is nice because you know it'll feel good to warm them up."

"I don't like cold feet."

"Well, I do." I say and cross my arms.

She lifts one eyebrow and leans back in her creaky chair. "One more time, I hate my feet being cold. Unless it's about doing something I don't want to do. Then yeah, I could get cold feet."

I let her words thwap around in my brain, trying to decide what she means. "Is that a *threat?*"

"*I do not want to be cold.*"

"Fine. I hear you." My voice sounds as ungracious as I feel. I could give her a few other things to worry about. Real worries, lifted from my own list.

"Do you, though?"

I pull a deep breath into my lungs. I'd asked her for her biggest worry. It didn't matter what I thought about it. "Okay, we won't let you be cold, then."

She looks at me suspiciously. "You can't just say that. What, you're going to fix all Kiwi housing?"

If it's a challenge she's throwing at me, I don't blame her, since that's the fastest way to get me to commit to something. "I *can* just say that. We'll keep you warm."

"Hmm." But she appears mollified.

And I have another thing to add to my list of things to figure out how to do.

A week passes. Then another. The questions are endless and unanswerable.

What should we take? Just a suitcase? All our books? What about furniture? Apparently, some people move overseas and ship a full cargo container of possessions with them. I imagine them on their flights, tugging a cargo ship behind them on a string like a child's toy boat. But the most expensive pieces of furniture we own are the couch and two matching oversized living room chairs that we got for a total of three hundred dollars on Craigslist ten years ago. They looked shabby when we got them, and they haven't gotten spiffier. Might as well leave all the furniture behind.

We'll have to take *some* things, though, won't we? We can't afford to buy everything new in New Zealand. We'll need to take our favorite cooking pans and clothes. What about sheets, though? Are New Zealand beds the same sizes as American beds? (I google. They are not.) What about my buckwheat sleeping pillows? My standing desk? Lala's glass case of action figures and her gazillion board games?

Honestly, my favorite possessions are the electric appliances that make life easier and more pleasant. The cat litter robot that actually works, no scooping. The heated bidet seat on our toilet. The BedJet that heats our sheets to exactly the right temperature. (Yes, it's embarrassing. And awesome.) We are so *comfortable*. We have literally everything we need and want. But none of these favorite things will work on New Zealand voltage, and it's not as easy as plugging in a converter. We'd need a step-down transformer for each, which are big and bulky and hundreds of dollars.

So what, we're going to choose to rip ourselves from comfort and nosedive into difficulty? Of course I've heard that discomfort is where the growth happens, but who says I need to grow? I'm good! I'm happy as I am! Why fix what ain't broke? We can still change our minds!

My heart whispers: *Grow*.

Chapter 3

Where Are the Grown-Ups?

In front of the U-Haul store, Lala and I step out of my car and gaze up at the orange sign. As we take our first shaky steps forward, I reach for Lala's hand. She squeezes back. My sweaty hand is slick in hers.

Then we enter.

We buy moving boxes.

Okay, confession: we only buy five book boxes and five small boxes. We say this is because we're not sure how many boxes will fit in my Smart car. But the truth is we're still scared. We need a grown-up to tell us how to do this. There's no way *we* can be the grown-ups.

At home, I fill the first box with books. My hands tremble as the tape screeches off its roll. I seal the lid, not to be opened until we're in a foreign country, in a new home I can't yet visualize. I don't even know how to get the box there, wherever *there* ends up being.

Shit, I don't even know how to get *us* there yet.

We now only have five and a half months to enter New Zealand, but pandemic red tape is keeping us from buying plane tickets.

To enter New Zealand, it's not enough to be a New Zealand citizen, partner, child, or critical worker. There are also fourteen mandatory days of quarantine to go through in specialized hotels set up near major airports. We can't buy a plane ticket to New Zealand unless we can prove we've booked a quarantine hotel reservation.

But—no surprise—all the expat Kiwis are trying to leave the pandemic-riddled countries they've been living in and get home. Every time the Managed Isolation and Quarantine (MIQ) hotels open new slots, they're snapped up in minutes. I join a Facebook group that posts when anyone sees spaces, but even that doesn't help. The demand is just too high.

I'm complaining about this to Lala one afternoon in my office. "Look, I'll show you." I pull up the site, log in, and click on the calendar. "All those red boxes? Those days are all full. And you never see—"

You never see green boxes.

There's a green box.

"Is that an open date?" asks Lala.

I've looked at this page a thousand times. This is my first green box sighting. "It can't be."

"Looks open to me."

"Holy crap. But—it's for July. We don't have to enter until end of August." I hear what I'm saying, and so does Lala.

"Should we book it?"

I have no air in my lungs. "And leave in four months? Is that even possible?"

"I don't know. Is it?"

"How are we supposed to decide that?" *Where is the grown-up we can ask?*

Lala shrugs and I feel the motion of her shoulders in the

pit of my soul. I move my computer mouse in small circles. I hit Reserve just to see what it will ask me.

After several clicks and two tick boxes that say I understand what I'm reserving, we have an MIQ slot. We also have a code that I can now enter at Air New Zealand to buy plane tickets.

I suck in a breath. All my courage has pooled in the bottoms of my feet, and before it drains away entirely, we look at Air New Zealand's seat selection for one of the two flights a week that leave from San Francisco.

"Holy shit," I breathe, as I click the Buy button. Next to me, Lala's breathing is as shallow as my own.

One-way tickets.

Purchased.

Time then passes at both a gallop and a standstill.

Four months to go. Then three and a half.

I pack boxes. Lala packs boxes. We yell at each other at least once a day about where the packing tape is, until I buy a ten-pack. And even then, we can never find the tape guns. We haven't done this together before, not once. When we bought this house fifteen years ago, we moved into it together from our separate apartments.

Turns out that moving sucks donkey balls.

Our house has exploded into boxes and piles of things to make decisions about. So. Many. Piles. Of. Things. So many decisions. What do we take? What do we sell or donate?

We've finally decided *how* to get our things to New Zealand. Using a company that ships single pallets of goods around the world, we'll put one pallet, or one hundred cubic feet of goods, on a ship. This isn't much at all. It's a cube about four and a half feet wide. Trying to cull a very full, eleven-hundred-square-foot, three-bedroom house into just what fits onto one pallet is an intense feat of advanced decision-making. With that in mind, we hold things in our hands, and even if they spark so much joy they cough up little rainbows, we still have to contort ourselves into judges, handing down life-and-death verdicts. We won't bring a single drinking glass that doesn't have a truly delightful story attached to it. Lala's butt-ugly octopus fruit bowl is spared the death sentence and will come with us, god help us all.

My beloved rolltop desk can't come, obviously. We're bringing no furniture except my hope chest, which is, after all, just another box to fill. So I sell my cherished desk to a woman who says she's a cousin of Emily Dickinson six times removed. When she arrives to pick it up, she's so annoying with her screeches of joy and unwelcome hugs that I hope she's lying about the Emily connection. I feel terrible for betraying my desk, and battle back both tears and the words *You can't have it.* Nausea rises as I watch her van drive away, and when I viciously stub my toe on my way into the house, I'm glad for the excuse to cry.

We pack. And we pack.

And we get rid of things.

It turns out that my Smart car can hold approximately eleventy billion boxes and bags. Normally, I wouldn't darken the Salvation Army's doors, as they hate the gays and offer "conversion" help, but apparently the combination of the pandemic and the launch of the television show *The Home Edit* means that the thrift stores in the Bay Area have mostly stopped taking donations of any kind. The Salvation

Army is the only exception to this, and yes, I *will* betray my morals to rid myself these of mountains of objects, books, and clothes.

The guy who works the bins at the back of the downtown Oakland Salvation Army gets the biggest kick out of seeing what I can pull out of my car. He calls his guys out of the warehouse every time I pull up. "She's here! Come look at this chick and her car! You're not gonna believe this! How does she *do* this, man?"

It's easier for me than for Lala, this decluttering. I love pretty things and books and yarn and candles, but getting rid of things has always given me a sweet, sharp high. I read about minimalism like it's porn, something to keep hidden in the (cluttered) bedside drawer. Fantasies better not acted on, but titillating all the same.

It's much harder for Lala. She's a pack rat and lover of objects, a save-it-just-in-case kind of person. Once upon a time, she will tell you, she had a ticket to see Prince. When he canceled the show, the tickets were still valid for the next year's show. But Lala's was lost in an accidental throw-out, and she *says* this is why she keeps old twist ties and cords that haven't been plugged in to anything for decades. But since visiting her father's (*ahem*) cluttered home, I look at her groaning shelves and think about apples and trees.

Something Lala has missed in lockdown is going to Target, just to look at things. "Stuff," she says. "Stuff and things. I miss *items*." Her office holds much more than it should be able to, as if she's bent space somehow over the years. Each item is precious to her, with its own story and import. Leaving behind things she loves is breaking her heart. With difficulty, she's culled art supplies and action figures, musical instruments and electronics.

But when she decides not to bring most of her comic

books, the look on her face as she chooses what to let go makes me want to weep.

I ask as gently as I can, "Do you want me to take them to the thrift store for you?" We've already sold all the books that we could to used bookshops, including online. No one wants these ones, not even the trade paperback omnibuses.

She nods, unable to meet my eyes. I take her boxes, and she retreats into her office, shutting the door with a quiet click.

At the back of the Salvation Army, I get in the drive-through line again. Two cars can pull up at the same time, allowing their drivers to dump unwanted possessions into huge bins marked Books, or Kitchen, or Furniture. The boss sees my car in line and hollers for his workers to come out and ogle how much I'll pull out of my car this time.

I check out the car in front of me. The woman is cheerfully upending box after box into the bins. Her partner, on the other hand, is peering into the bins with a hopeful look on his face. And he is a *nerd*. He's wearing a Commander Shepard hoodie (Lala has one just like it), and there's a *Deep Space Nine* bumper sticker on the back of their car.

"Hey," I call to him. "Do you like comics?"

His whole face brightens, but this is the big city, so his voice is careful. "Why?"

"We're moving to New Zealand. My wife has to get rid of all of hers."

"Really? Can I see?" His voice isn't careful anymore, and as he pokes through the boxes, it's clear he desperately wants every single one.

I help him carry them to his car, where his partner is *pissed*. "Are you serious? This was our weekend to get *rid* of stuff. Not to bring home more!"

I feel no remorse, and it's obvious he doesn't either. We

pantomime giving each other a giddy high five and then we drive away.

At home, I tell Lala I didn't have to pour her comics into a giant book bin.

Her gratitude is a paper cut sliced across my heart.

With only two months to go, we've finally finished most of the clearing out.

Now, the plan is to finish packing the rest of the house this weekend. Then we'll get rid of everything that's left, except a few essential pieces of furniture that will stay in place until the very last minute—our bed, our couch, the dining table, two chairs. My voice echoes and bounces off the empty walls. Lala isn't a fan of my new minimalist intercom.

On Monday, our handyperson will come in and fix all the things and paint the interior. Jose has already painted the yellow exterior an excruciatingly boring pale gray that's apparently all the rage. Embarrassment floods us every time we pull up in front of the house. We aren't gray people! We are yellow people! We love reds! Oranges! This gray paint is called "San Francisco Fog," but actual fog has way more personality than this chalky ash color.

After Jose covers the interior yellow and orange walls with a similarly popular and equally dispiriting gray or bisque or pearl, we'll get the bedrooms recarpeted, hire the inspection, and get the staging done. The house we've lived in will go up for sale, taking with it a sizable chunk of our hearts. That said, we're hoping it will sell quickly in this market that people are constantly telling us is hot-hot-*hot,* although the idea of a superheated market is enough to make my stomach hurt.

And then what?

We don't know. We'll be in some weird limbo while the house is for sale—someone's coming to see it? Run away! But it's still a pandemic! Hide someplace safe! Then, if it sells before we depart, will we be able to rent back from the new owner until we move? Will we find an Airbnb? Squat in the unoccupied downstairs unit at my sister's apartment building?

I drop into bed every night exhausted, my lids fluttering shut, only to snap open a few minutes later as my lists of undone things flash in my brain like neon tequila signs on a dark back road. The sheer *gall* of what we're doing washes over me in cold waves at least a couple of times a day.

One night, Lala goes out to jam with some musician friends. When she gets home, she says, "Diana said we were really brave."

Diana is a smart woman, and I agree with her. But Lala's face looks weird—almost confused—so I say, "Well, yeah. Don't you think it takes bravery to move halfway around the world?"

"I don't know! I hadn't really thought about it!"

Surprise rockets through my chest. "Oh, my god, it's *all* I think about. You haven't been scared?"

She pales. "Not until *now,* no! I was only worried about being cold!"

Great.

Now we're both terrified.

For the last three days, I've been practicing keeping Lala warm, heating the house way past my comfort level. I spend most of my waking hours in my office, and if I close my door and cover the heating vent with a collection of blankets and pillows, I can keep my office as cool as the side of a refrigerator while the rest of the house shimmers like a desert road in the sun.

Lala finally realizes the house has been consistently warm enough for her to wear just a T-shirt, no sweatshirt needed. "You've been running the heat more than you usually do."

I smile. "Are you warm enough?"

Instead of being grateful, she says, "Are you being passive-aggressive?"

Please. As if.

Okay, I'm not above being passive-aggressive on a bad day. But in this case, I'm not. "You will *not* be cold in New Zealand. If we have to buy three space heaters and sit you in the middle of them all winter long, you won't be cold. I've been trying to demonstrate that I'm serious about this promise."

"You've been heating the house for one day!"

"*Three* days," I correct her. "And remember, we won't rent a place unless we're confident that the heat pump works. Whatever that is."

Here's the thing: we both want to go to New Zealand. We both think it's a good idea. So many people want to go, but we're actually able to. But our fears are big and real, and what I have to remember is every time I downplay one of her fears, I'm not listening to the person I chose to spend my life with. I'm not listening to the person I'm in love with. That's not okay. So in this late Oakland winter, I will continue to wear a tank top and shorts inside in order to reassure Lala that she never has to be cold again.

With each box I close and each bag I discard, I'm dismantling the life I've so carefully built. I lose my breath at least once a day, shocked by the brutal blow of it.

When will we be home again?

I keep the fan pointed directly at my face, and I cross off the days on my printed out calendar. For the thousandth time, I reread Anaïs Nin's quote I've written at the bottom of the page: "Life shrinks or expands in proportion to one's courage."

I haven't printed out the blank months that come after the move yet. I'm not sure when—or even if—I will.

Chapter 4

This Is Not My Beautiful House

In the dim light of the hotel corridor, I swipe the hotel key card. Red light. I swipe it again. Red light.

Fuck.

"You want me to try?" Lala asks.

I do *not*. I can do it myself. One more time, and the light goes green, thank god. I'm so exhausted I can't imagine dragging myself and my suitcase back down to the lobby to get the card recoded.

The hotel is just five miles from our home, right next to the Oakland airport. We're so close to the tarmac that the walls rumble as planes pass overhead. We're not here because of the proximity to the airport—we're here because the hotel's reviews on Yelp did not suck and because we're escaping our house, which has been torn to bits.

At home, the inside walls are still tacky with fresh paint, and today, men are laying down white carpet and laminate over our old, scratched wooden floors. My heart cramps at the thought of our gorgeous hardwood being covered up. It's antithetical to everything I love in an almost-hundred-year-old house. Laminate is the polar opposite of character.

We've even hired a stager, something I thought I'd never do. Pay thousands of dollars to bring in an interior designer and cold, bland furniture? But the cold, bland look is what people want and are paying top dollar for, so we're doing everything our realtor tells us. Last night we slept on an air mattress in our bedroom, trying desperately to avoid touching the freshly painted walls. The very *idea* of the white carpet going in today leaves me feeling strung out like a house cat stuck outside in a hailstorm, so a hotel it is.

We trundle our stuff in, odd vagabonds carrying bits of our life's circus. Yes, we each have a suitcase, but we also have strange things we didn't want to leave in the house: my ukulele; Lala's banjo and PlayStation.

"I'm going to do it," I say to my wife.

She rolls her eyes. "I know you are."

Relief loosens the taut nerves at the back of my neck. I know it makes Lala feel dirty—my little habit. She'd never do it, not a chance in hell.

But I have to.

I pull open a drawer under the TV and sigh. *Oh, yeah.* My fingers tingle. I stack the restaurant suggestions on top of the Bible and get ready to do my favorite thing.

I unpack.

Gently, I slide folded T-shirts and jeans into the dresser. Underwear and bras get their own neat little stack. My dresses hang in the closet. My three pairs of shoes line up underneath, their toes in tidy formation.

We're here for a few days, but even if I'm only in a hotel for a single night, this is what I do. Confession: I even unpack in tents when we go camping. It's not like I have a closet or a chest of drawers in there, but I use the space next to my side of the blow-up air mattress to make orderly stacks. (They should *totally* make blow-up camping bureaus for people like me. We would buy the hell out of them.)

I need to know where my things are, and that's because I'm a nester to the core. While I don't really believe in astrology, I love that my Cancerian crab carries its shell. How lovely to be a crab. When you open your eyes? At home. Close them at night, having scuttled many miles? Still at home.

We had a toy box growing up, and at any given time, I was the biggest toy in the box. To me, the box felt spacious, but it couldn't have been more than two or three feet wide, made of red and blue slatted wood. If I slid my legs in first and arranged myself just so, I could wriggle my way in, pulling the toys and blankets and stuffed animals around me like so many high-thread-count sheets and down comforters. The goal was to get far enough in that I could have both my neck *and* my book supported and then, let me tell you, it was heaven in a box. If it'd had wheels, I'm sure I would have thump-rolled my way all over the house, a girl-shaped hermit crab.

I have a fond spot for hermit crabs, those home-away-from-home arthropods. Crabs in general delight me. The Dungeness, is of course, delicious. The coconut crab is majestic in its fearsome size, forty inches tip to tip, the adults weighing ten pounds. Their pincers can apply seven hundred pounds of force and can crush the coconuts they're named for.

But I love best the hermit crabs and their Goldilocks dance. They don't build their own shells—they inhabit old, discarded mollusk shells. That means as they grow, they're always on the lookout for better digs. If Sully the Hermit Crab is on its way to the cafe and spies a nice-looking empty shell, it'll skitter out of its own, and slip its naked body into the new shell to see if it's a better fit. If so, huzzah! It leaves the old shell on the roadside like rubber from a blown-out tire and goes on its merry way to pick up a mocha frappé.

If the vacant shell doesn't fit, however, the hermit crab slides back into its old one. Then it gives up on the idea of coffee. It sits and waits. Other hermit crabs notice this little guy and the vacant shell. They also try on the glass slipper, and if it doesn't fit, they go back to their shell and wait with Sully. Eventually, one of the crabs who tries on the shell will do a happy dance and show off how great it makes his calves look. He's keeping it!

At that moment, all the other crabs who've been waiting for this magical moment hop out of their shells and into the next size bigger. Ideally, everyone gets a better house! In reality, some of them duke it out, but it generally works well for all involved.

This social structure is called a vacancy chain, and it's not just for crabs. We see it happen whenever a vacancy enters a population, like when a job is created or when a new house is built. Someone moves into the new spot, and those below move upward into something that's hopefully a better fit.

But I worry about the hermit crabs. On the surface it seems fabulous—each crab in the vacancy conga line gets a new shell. The last abandoned shell is left behind. Everyone's happy. Right?

What if it's harder than it looks? Do shells take a while to get used to? Do they rub, like a new shoe scrapes the back of an ankle? Does Sully miss the smell of its old shell? Does the new place have curtains yet? Does the sun wake up a newly moved hermit crab at five-thirty every morning? Can the crab still hang out with their old neighbors, or do their friends forget them as soon as the cool new neighbor moves in?

Do they ever regret leaping out of their cozy shell and hurtling their soft, naked body through the cold water to try on something terrifying and new?

Do hermit crabs like David Byrne? Do they constantly sing, as I do: *And you may find yourself in another part of the world...And you may ask yourself, "Well, how did I get here?"*

As I unpack in the hotel with its vacancy sign glowing outside our curtain, I understand that the point of my fretting about the vacancy chain is control. Of course it is.

If I know what item I possess, and where it is, and what it's used for, then maybe I have some kind of authority over my life. Bonus points if I know how the item could be used outside its normal function. Like, that roll of twisted clothesline is great for hanging up wet swimsuits, but it could also be a bungee cord to strap a zombie onto the top of the car. Duct tape wrapped around a pencil makes a good finger-rest, but it also comes in handy *for almost everything* including taping up broken airplane wings. Duct tape will probably save my life at some point.

Okay, yeah, did you notice that? I went from duct tape's utility to survival worry without passing Go, without collecting two hundred dollars.

My desperate desire for control, even if it's simply about folding T-shirts into an extra-small packing cube, always comes down to one base emotion: *fear*.

Even as I'm cracking jokes about it, I'm scared.

Some strange people feel only exhilaration at a lack of constancy. But the rest of us—instead of opening our hands to accept the chaos of life, we clench them in an attempt to hold onto what we have as hard as we can. Fear looks different for different people—some rage, others hide. Some people collect things, scared they won't have enough. Others tidy obsessively, scared they won't keep what they have. Honestly, I understand both urges.

The average American home holds about 300,000 items. We can't possibly control or understand or remember what those things even are.

So on one hand, our house being tossed like a salad is stressing me the hell out.

On the other hand, culling all our possessions for the move, jettisoning stuff out of our nest, while difficult, is calming me down, because all of a sudden, I *do* know what I have.

And you may say to yourself, My God! What have I done?

What I've gotten rid of: almost everything.

I've purged my books, my clothes, my shoes, my pens. Furniture. Lamps. Salad spinners. That fondue pot we never used, not even once. I've gotten rid of yarn and photos, and did I mention books? So many books. I threw out the toilet plunger, and the next day, I asked Lala to get another one from Target. We normally don't need one, but what if we *did*? Ack. We still have to sell this house, after all.

While un-nesting, I've attempted to be ruthlessly unsentimental.

For years, I'd kept my mother's piano sheet music. It was tattered, literally falling apart in my hands when I touched it. Yellowed Chopin nocturnes and brittle Mozart serenades rested against old German collections of hymns and love songs.

Me? If a piece has more than one flat or two sharps, I can't play it, which means I'm restricted to C, D, F, and G major. Even if I attempt to play a song in one of those keys, it has to be simple. I can work both hands at the same time, but it's not pretty. At forty-eight years old, becoming proficient on the piano is not something I want to do in this lifetime. Neither do my sisters, who don't play at all.

But as I packed that corner of the living room bookcase one night, as I paged through the scrappy leaves of soft paper, my chest tightened in pain. At the top of each piano piece, my mother had written her name in soft pencil, now smudged. *Janette Ashcroft.* It was funny—none of them said her "adult" married name, Jan Herron. These books and sheets were from her youth. I was never going to use them. I checked to see if they were rare or worth anything, monetarily, and they were not.

How do you throw away your mother's handwritten maiden name?

Presumably, she'd sat in front of these pieces for hours. Had she struggled to get her fingers into the right places at the right times, her body swaying gently as the notes came easier with practice? Had the pages absorbed the energy of a woman who was decades from meeting her daughters?

Paper is heavy. And paper that will never be useful again is somehow heavier.

So, with an equally leaden heart, I placed them in the city-managed compost bin. Mom would have liked that part, at least. Those pages, including her penciled marks, would turn into something else that would promote growth somewhere, someday.

Even so, throwing them out *hurt*. They had lined part of my nest for so long, and my nest was thinning every day.

I also got rid of the last of the love letters.

A long time ago, I tossed the problematic ones, the ones from people who didn't treat me well. But for some reason, I'd held onto some from good, kind people, from the relationships that just didn't work out.

Why was I keeping them, anyway? When I held them in my hands, the handwriting made my stomach drop. How *well* I knew those bits of script, those inked marks, that slant on the *L* or the cross on the *T*, that used to heat my cheeks and make my heart race.

Now, they did nothing for me. Words extolling my best qualities as a twenty- or thirty-something mean little now. I'm not the same person. Those notes held no revelation, and in some cases, they held pain. I found a series of Post-it notes in an envelope. One said, "A pair of good socks from Neiman Marcus. I have at least forty." Another said, "One breakfast at the Grill. Hopefully you'll be in the booth with me and not working." Another: "A new hardcover. I've got a hundred I haven't read." I was confused until a dim memory rang a quiet bell: each Post-it had been stuck to a twenty-dollar bill. I'd been her waitress, broke and living in a falling-down shack. She'd been a rich, middle-aged yuppie with a Jack London loft and money to burn. I'd taken those twenties I'd been unable to refuse, peeling off and saving the Post-its, both loving and hating her for her generosity. We'd been in love, then she broke my heart. Many years later, she died.

I put the Post-its in the recycling bin.

I found two very long letters from a boy I'd had *such* a

crush on, a smart boy who snuck girls into the monastery where he rented a room during college. I wanted to be one of those girls, but before that could happen, I moved to Oakland. He went to New York. His letters were hip and funny and chatty. In the second one, at the bottom of the last page, he wrote, "You know I moved here with Sarita, right?" I hadn't known. I didn't write him back after that.

I googled him, and an old man with his name popped onto my screen. Lord have mercy, that person couldn't be *him*—but there he was, still in the town where we'd met. I emailed him, asking if he wanted the letters back. They were long and journal-like, lost thoughts of his that I currently owned, thoughts I could give back.

He responded enthusiastically. *I'd dig seeing them, but are you sure you can part with them (you can always make xeroxes)*. I was pretty sure he was kidding about the xeroxing, and I popped the originals into the mail.

The love of my life, the one with whom I'm dismantling our nest, doesn't write me letters. I don't need them. I have her.

What I kept: potential.

I kept most of my unread books. Hundreds of them. One of them might change my life when I get around to reading it, and books are much more expensive in New Zealand than they are in the States. Into boxes they went.

I kept knitting projects, the projects that I loved but hadn't yet finished, and the projects I was obsessed with but hadn't yet started. It was easier to give away hand knits where the yarn's potential for awesomeness had already morphed into an actual sweater, where I was able to say, *No, this shoulder doesn't fit me well.* I parted with bags of sweaters and shawls I never wore, leaving me with just seven sweaters to send around the world.

While I'm more obsessively tidy than Lala, I'm not far behind her in being able to fit an astonishing number of things into small, hidden spaces. I wouldn't be surprised if we owned more than the average bear when we started purging and packing.

But now? We're down to sixty-seven boxes (most of them are one cubic foot, the small kind made for books). I could take a wild guess and say that most of the boxes hold twenty-five things each. Many hold fewer, I know. That means we're down to no more than 1,675 items that are being shipped over on a couple of pallets, a far cry from that average 300,000.

We're also each taking two thirty-one-inch suitcases with us on the plane. I'd estimate we'll be bringing one or two hundred things with us in those. Of course, it's almost impossible to quantify—fifty hairbands take up less room than one shoe.

But I know this: we're down from owning well over a quarter-million items to a couple of thousand.

The nest I've loved so much for fifteen years is now completely unlined. The house is hollow. The closets are empty. Every piece of furniture we've ever owned has been carried away except for the mid-century modern record cabinet, the only piece that was judged good enough to be allowed to stay as part of the staging (our pajama-clad neighbor Megan will inherit it after we leave).

This is not my beautiful house. How did I get here?

I finish unpacking into the hotel's drawers. "There. I put my suitcases in the back of the closet."

Lala just nods. I feel a pulse of gratitude that she always lets me do my own thing, that she couldn't care less where I store my suitcases while we're here.

Last week, we had an impromptu gathering at our house. It was physically awkward, since we were between the hours of the trash removal van that came to get the last of our junk and the time when the stager would come to measure the space.

Sweat covered me, and not the pretty, glowy kind. It was panic sweat, the smelly kind. We had no chairs at all, except for a few outdoor ones that my sister was going to take away with her. I'd been racing around all day, carrying things from one place to another, my feet aching with the twenty-three thousand steps I'd get that day.

Suddenly, our friend Jodi turned up to give us hugs. My little sister Bethany arrived at the same time to pick up our yard furniture. Megan materialized wearing Tabasco PJs. The five of us sat outside in mismatched furniture, Bethany perching on the porch steps.

As we chatted, I tried to hide my tension and be in the moment. "Yeah," I said. "We're excited. Looking forward to staying in the North Island for a while, then we might go to —oh, *shit,* Lala! We have to check that little closet next to the pantry! Did you clean that out? Did I? Do we have any more contractor bags? *Why* isn't the stager here yet? Oh, god, did we give Jose the final check?"

In the same voice she would use to say that it was warm outside, my sister noted, "It's like you're possessed."

Lala just kept her eyes on her phone as she scrolled, looking for something she wanted to show Jodi.

I ignored my sister. My brain was cacophonous, and I suddenly realized something vitally important that had to be said before I forgot. "Lala."

She grunted, her eyes still on her phone.

"If you want to divorce me, now's the time."

"Mmmm." She kept scrolling. "That's okay."

My sister and friends, on the other hand, looked horrified.

But it made perfect sense to me. "We're liquid. Or at least we're going to be when we sell the house." I leaned forward. "If we're going to break up, now's the time. We could just write a check and be done."

"Okay. But I'm good," said Lala, then she showed her phone to Jodi, sharing the cat video she'd been searching for.

I think our witnesses remained a little shaken, but I loved her answer. In the turmoil and loss of control, inside the fear, we continue to choose each other.

Now, in our hotel room, we hear the planes roar overhead, the hotel's walls shaking with each approach and takeoff. While some rooms probably have a view of the air traffic, we look out on a dumpster, which is for the best, really. Every time I see an airplane, I'm reminded that soon, we'll climb into one and leave this country behind.

We've never been so untethered. So very un-nested.

At that thought, fear quakes through me.

What are we *doing*? Every few days, I look around and wonder how we got to this point. Obviously, we made a choice, and then we put one foot in front of the other. We knew this was where we were heading, but to be almost at the point of casting off the ropes that hold the balloon to the earth is a fucking *trip*.

My first adult tethers came at eighteen, when I got my first credit card. Even though I worked up to four part-time jobs at a time while putting myself through college, I owed a significant amount of money to my credit cards and my undergrad alma mater by the time I graduated at twenty-five.

I moved on to grad school, and by twenty-seven, I owed a shit-ton, thanks to grad-school debt. Waitressing wasn't paying the bills, so I got a job dispatching 911.

At thirty-two, still deep in debt, I bought a condo and all the stress a mortgage brings.

At thirty-four, I married Lala and we bought our house. I sold my first book and worked two jobs (writing and dispatching) for the next ten years. We finally started to pay off the debt, slowly and doggedly.

At forty-four, I left 911 to write full time. By then, we'd dug our way out of debt except for the house, but that three-grand mortgage bill still came due each month. We weren't going anywhere. The mortgage had to be paid.

Yesterday, I turned off the mortgage auto-payment. We've made the last installment we'll ever make on our home.

Since the age of eighteen, I've been strapped to working, strapped to debt, strapped to a *job*.

Now we're strapped to absolutely nothing, or we will be if the house sale goes through. We'll have no debt at all. Soon, we'll have no house. We'll sell our two cars. We'll just have two suitcases. A mere sixty-seven boxes of books and yarn and Lala's favorite action figures will soon be bobbing over the ocean.

Lala lies next to me on the hotel bed. She's hooked up her PlayStation to the TV, and her eyes are glued to the screen as she plays *Assassin's Creed*. Tinny music bleeds from her headphones.

I press my side against hers. She pats my leg and smiles before focusing again on her game. Idly, I watch her play—the game is set in Venice, and I recognize the squares her character runs through even though the game is set in 1509. She leaps from a church's spire down to the cobblestones below, and I know that just around the corner from where she lands is an osteria that has amazing meatballs. (It probably served the same ones in the sixteenth century too.)

In the game, the water of the lagoon gleams, and I see two crabs scuttling along the edge of a fishing net.

I look at the hotel room's closet doors, behind which rest my two suitcases and my neatly lined-up shoes. I love a nest, be it a house or tent or hotel room. I love unpacking into it and making it mine.

Could it be possible I don't *need* one?

Another plane shakes the building, and Lala and I remain side by side, two hermit crabs who still want to share the same view.

Same as it ever was. Same as it ever was.

Chapter 5

An Attempt to Inventory Fear

Our house sells in five days. The money hits our bank account, giving me a cheerful but startling jolt every time I open our banking app.

With two weeks until our departure, we've taken up residence in an Oakland Airbnb, a nice two-bedroom apartment with a charming veranda where we can pick plums and figs without even bending over the rail.

And I'm having trouble breathing some mornings.

I'm so fucking scared.

So simple, those words. I'm not sure people really understand what I mean when I say them.

A friend asks, "How are you doing with the whole moving thing?"

"I'm terrified."

My friend laughs, the audible equivalent of a pat on the head, and the subject quickly changes to other topics: the thriller she's reading and what she's going to be teaching in the fall.

That's fine. I can't expose the true depth of the fear, not

really. I don't know how to articulate what it feels like. (I just sat here for a minute, my fingers hovered over my keyboard, trying to find the words. While I did, I chewed four fingernails right down to the quick. I don't think I've done that in thirty years.)

I can't explain this liquid lake of fear that's replaced all my blood.

I am a knower.

I am a planner.

But in this moment, two weeks before we leave America for good, I know nothing, and because of that, I have almost nothing planned.

We don't even know what city we'll be in after we land. Okay, our plane's wheels will touch down in Auckland, but we'll be met by the military, then every single passenger will be put onto buses. Only after we're on board the bus will we be told in what town we'll do our fourteen-day quarantine. It could be Auckland, or Rotorua, or we could be put on another plane and sent to the South Island. It's at the government's discretion, based on what quarantine hotels have room available. We only know that we'll be in a hotel *somewhere* in New Zealand for fourteen days, unable to leave the room.

After we get out (provided we haven't murdered each other), we have no plans. None.

Will we be digital nomads, moving from town to town on the weekends, settling down in rentals during the week to do our work? That's the tentative plan, yes.

Or maybe we'll hate that immediately and do something else. (What would that be? No clue.)

We don't even know what island we'll eventually settle on, let alone what city. How can we choose when we've never lived in any city in New Zealand? At this point we're drawn to Christchurch because it's a foodie city and affordable, but who knows?

Sitting in the office of this apartment, my racing mind can't tackle one anxious thought before the next one barges in. The worries frighten me so much that my soul simply takes off all its clothes and goes to lie down on the highway. It can't handle this, any of it. Without a soul, I'm left dry-mouthed at the computer, a vacant-eyed husk with admittedly very cute glasses.

This fear is hollowing me out, and I'm not sure what will fill the void left behind.

I recently heard Tim Ferriss speak about fear on his podcast, in which he shared an exercise called Fear Setting. Yes, it sounded privileged to me too. Most people don't get to set intentions around doing hard things. They just have to *do* them. This move? We don't have to do it. We're privileged that way.

That acknowledged, it sounded like a valid exercise, and one that I did *not* want to do. Therefore, I knew I should probably do it.

So today, I will sit down at the Airbnb desk to make the list that will undoubtedly solve all my fears. Yes, it's a bit late for this kind of exercise. Our house is sold, the plane tickets bought. But hell, we can still decide to move to Boise if the exercise goes badly enough.

I pick up my pen and take the first step, writing down my fears.

. . .

A Few Fears About Moving to New Zealand

- That someone I love will die and I won't get home in time to say goodbye.
- That I'll start crying when I leave my sisters and never stop. That missing them will kill me.
- That we won't be able to make deep, nourishing friendships in a new place.
- That we won't be able to make enough money to survive there.
- That Lala will hate working her job remotely.
- That we'll be homesick all the time.
- That I'll never sell a book again and no one will want to take my classes, and we'll be broke.

These are just the biggest fears on my list. By the time I finish writing all of them, big and small, I'm clammy and queasy. The *what the hell are we doing* refrain starts up again in my head.

Now I'm supposed to write a list of how I will prevent those things. Next to that, I'll write a list of how I can repair the calamities I fear if they come to pass.

Oooh! This part is made for me! I'm a preventer and a repairer as well as a planner and a worrier. This is where I'll figure it all out. Yep, these are some scary fears! Thank goodness I now have a tool to help!

I take my pencil to the Prevent column with high hopes.

My first fear: that someone will die without me getting to say goodbye. What's the prevention for that?

I push another See's candy—a gift from my sister—into my mouth as I frown toward the ceiling. Tim Ferriss says to list the prevention that you can take. So there has to be at least one prevention. Right?

But—if the person I love dies out of the blue, and I don't get there in time to tell them I love them, how the hell do I prevent *that*?

The only thing I can think of is to call each and every person I love every day and tell them how much they mean to me. While it's a charming thought, I have a nice long list of loved ones and not enough time.

Is this tool broken?

I skip ahead to the Repair column.

So, how would I repair something like that? My loved one would be dead. I do not dabble with necromancy.

This shit is broken. Stupid Tim Ferriss.

In disgust, I skip down to some of the lighter worries, where I manage to write a few ideas in the Prevent and Repair columns. If the fear has to do with money, we can budget and save. In case of total financial catastrophe, we can always—worst case—come back to the States and live with family. For the friendship fears, I brainstorm ways to make friends and how to stay connected to my friends in the States.

But my eyes keep returning to that top fear, the unpreventable one, the irreparable one. And something about it feels so very familiar. Déjà vu prickles along my skin. Where have I felt this before?

Oh, yes.

In recovery.

When I got sober, I worked through the twelve steps with my sponsor. As a lifelong suck-up A student, I loved this part of recovery, the part that had worksheets and homework, things that I could try to do "right."

Back then, I did a fear inventory. I listed all my fears,

from painful death to big gusts of wind. If it scared me, it went on the list.

Then my sponsor and I talked about what I could do about those fears.

The answer?

Nothing.

I had no control.

I didn't have control over death. I didn't have control over wind. I had no control over other people's feelings, or even my own, a lot of the time. I had no control over other drivers on the road, no matter how tightly I gripped the steering wheel. I had no control over my wife, even though I definitely had *opinions* about the way she did almost everything.

"What's inside your hula hoop?" my sponsor asked me, over and over.

I squirmed in my seat, barely preventing myself from sticking my tongue out at her. "But Lala *can't* ride a motorcycle. She just can't. It's too dangerous."

"Wow. Your wife's a grown adult, right? How are you going to keep her from riding one?"

I practiced releasing control, a lot. If the thing I was upset about was inside my hula hoop (my body, my mind), I got to try to control it. If it was outside the range of my swinging hips, I didn't. After months of practice, and after years of telling my wife she couldn't ride a motorcycle, I bought Lala motorcycle lessons. I admit I hoped she would hate riding. Sadly, she didn't. She bought a motorcycle, which she never even once crashed. (A motorcycle which is too expensive to ship to New Zealand. I hate that I'm relieved by that.)

With each control-releasing practice session, I got a little better at it. Shockingly, life got better when I realized it wasn't up to me to make the world go around the correct way.

A weird feeling arose out of nowhere: calmness. A quiet stillness. Serenity. Yes, I still hated it when people shouted at their phones in public, but then I could just shrug and think about something else instead of steaming. People being stupid in traffic stopped bothering me at all. Even my own inability to cross everything off my To-Do list stopped stressing me out. I started to accept things as they actually were.

It's a work in progress, of course. Do I still want to control everything from the volume of the washing machine to what other people think about me? Yes! Of course I do!

Do I try to control those things? Sure, but way less than I used to.

And these things, these Very Big Scary Things that might happen because of moving to New Zealand—they're not things I can control.

Maybe no one will ever buy a book from me again. Perhaps someone I love will die. But those things could just as easily happen here in the States. A falling piece of space debris could strike any of us at any moment. Speaking of space trash, Jeff Bezos could decide books no longer work, and cancel them entirely. No one can predict the future. I can't even control the present when it's right in front of me.

At the desk, I pop another piece of See's candy into my mouth (I can control *that!*). I cast my eye over my Fear Setting list again.

Instead of stress working its way up my neck, something delicious flows through me.

There it is, that serenity again.

I can't do a single damn thing about anything on the list, not from where I'm sitting.

That means I can just let it all go.

All my worries are safe. They're chronicled, captured in one place. They don't need to go swimming through my mind at three in the morning anymore. I know where they are. If they have a prevention or a repair attached to them, I'll know where to find it. If they don't, well, that's just life.

At the end of Fear Setting, Tim says to write down the cost of inaction and rank it on a scale of 1-10.

I write: "If we don't move, we'll never know what we're capable of. We'll stay in Oakland with a mortgage we can't pay off before we retire. We'll live in a country neither of us feel safe in anymore. We won't have good health care. We won't adventure. We'll stagnate, growing angry and resentful."

I give that an ugly score of 2.

Then he says to write down the benefits of an attempt or partial success.

I write, "We see more of the world. We make new friends. We have more fun. We surprise ourselves. We live in wonder. We get comfortable with discomfort. We know each other better. We like each other even more. We like ourselves more. We're more comfortable being in the world. We feel free, not stuck. Choices are endless."

I give that a gorgeous score of 10, the only score it deserves.

Then I push myself away from the desk and walk through the house to give Lala a kiss where she sits at her computer. My shoulders are so light they float. The rewards, I have just proven, literally outweigh the risks, and I can't do anything about the risks right now, anyway.

"I like kisses," she says, smiling. "What's that for?"

"For wanting to go on this adventure with me." Just

saying it sets whispery wings of fear flapping in my chest again. That's okay. I can practice acceptance.

"That's me, the adventurer," she says cheerfully.

The night before, we'd had our big going away party. My band had learned the Chris Stapleton song about starting a new life with the one you love, and as a surprise, I'd sung it to Lala in front of all our friends. "Were you surprised when I sang 'Starting Over' for you?"

"Absolutely not."

I'm shocked. "What?"

"Do you know how often you play that song? And how you get all emotional when it comes on?"

"I didn't think you'd noticed."

She laughs. "You clutch my hand every time it comes on and say *This is the song for our move*. Yeah, I noticed."

I shrug. "I'm smooth."

"*So* smooth. So hard to read. Hey, you okay?"

"Yeah." The tears I've been holding back threaten to rise, so I swallow hard. Over Lala's shoulder, I see our four enormous suitcases, straining at their sides. "Still want to go?"

I want her to say, *Of course I do, darling. I'd go anywhere with you. You're all that matters in this adventure called life.* I want her to lean forward to take my face gently in her hands, her gaze raking across mine before planting a soft kiss on my lips.

Instead, she says, "What do you think?"

We're down to two suitcases each and we're leaving the country together. Her actions should be enough to show me all I need to know. A calm, sensitive, loving woman would sigh happily and press another kiss to her wife's lips.

Me, though: "God, just *say* it. I need to hear it."

At least the eye roll she gives is the gentle kind. "Yeah. I still want to go."

Mollified, I bat my eyelashes. "With me?"

"Who else would I go with?" she says. "You've got the magic passport."

Good point.

Lucky me.

Chapter 6

Trapped In a Very Small Room for a Very Long Time

Day Zero in Managed Isolation

I'm sitting in a chair in New Zealand, looking out a New Zealand window, watching a thin New Zealand rainstorm blow out of view.

Below the window is a pocket of hotel landscaping with lush greenery, palms, and bushes filled with small birds, but the glass is so thick I can't hear them chirping. Beyond the birds is a busy roadway in an industrial area where trucks frantically move shipping containers around.

We made it.

The flight was thirteen hours, which was shorter than the seventeen hours I'd been telling everyone it would be. I have no idea where I got that bigger number, but if you ever want to be relieved, overestimate the time you think your flight will take by four hours. We bought a "sky couch," which, in my mind, would be a chic little red settee where we'd be catered to by an airline hostess wearing a pillbox hat, selling cigarettes, and mixing cocktails. In reality, it was a three-seat section in coach with an unsold middle seat and a footrest that flipped up flat. It wasn't big enough for both of us to lie down in, but it was enough to couch-spoon in, which justified the extra expense.

So we're here! In New Zealand!

Except...I don't feel as if I'm really *in* New Zealand. I mean, the land the hotel rests upon is New Zealand soil, yes. But nothing is real, not yet. This is a liminal, middle ground.

Our whole plane was met by the Navy, rows of uniformed young people wearing tight fitting masks. We were tested for Covid-19. Then we claimed our bags, cleared customs, and, with the rest of the passengers, climbed onto buses. Some buses, we learned, were headed to downtown Auckland, and others left the city, southbound.

Our bus ride, though, was short, taking less than fifteen minutes, and we're now in a quarantine hotel near the Auckland airport. We'll stay here for our first fourteen days in the country.

Today is Day Zero. We'll get a second Covid-19 test soon, and if we're still negative, tomorrow will be day one of fourteen. If we remain negative, we'll be able to leave our rooms and walk in the fenced parking lot for forty-five minutes, once a day.

On day fourteen, we'll be released into the wild, into New Zealand proper. On day fourteen, we'll start our new lives.

My blood fizzes like soda. And I'm exhausted. It's nine in the morning, and I have to stay up till at least eight tonight to have a prayer of getting on local time quickly. So I stare at the black bird with the orange beak (common myna, my bird app says), and I take a deep breath of hotel-room air.

. . .

Day Two

I miss Dozy, who's staying with my best friend until we find a rental that will take dogs (not likely, says the internet) or buy a house. I'm trying not to think about her. When I do, I cry.

I have only blown up one extension cord and Lala has only lost one converter. Both emitted smoke and heat, but neither of them caught on actual fire or set off any smoke detectors. Yes, we understand voltage and amperage. For the most part. I simply like to forget on as many continents as possible that one should *never* use an extension cord from home. New Zealand, check! My curling iron works, though, and I'm calling that a big win.

Day Three

Our room is not glamorous. It's better than the one they originally put us in, which had nothing but two small beds and a chair. (No desk, no table, and lord help two full-sized women trying to fit into one double bed.) Had the front desk made a mistake? Had they seen two women with different last names and just assumed we weren't a couple? Or did all married couples share a smaller-than-queen bed here? I sent an email to the desk asking this, and they moved us to this room on the second day, thank *jeebus*. Both of us are working full time, and to do that without even a table to share felt dire.

The room they moved us to is the same size, about a hundred square feet, but it feels bigger with only one queen-sized bed in the middle of the floor instead of the two smaller beds. Bonus: we have one upholstered chair and one metal-legged chair that goes with the notebook-sized desk. The luxury of two places to sit that aren't on the bed!

It's so *quiet* here. We know we're surrounded on both sides and across the hall by other people in isolation, but we never see them. We don't even hear them. It's an airport hotel, so perhaps it's just very well soundproofed, but there are times I wouldn't mind hearing a voice or two filtering through a wall. I'd like to hear some proof that life is going on around us. Three times a day, someone knocks on the door and calls "Room Service!" but when we mask up and open the door to get the bags of food, that someone is already far down the hall and out of sight.

Day Five

We're traveling light for people moving around the globe, but we're not traveling *light*. We have nine pieces of luggage crammed in here with us: the four large suitcases and four backpacks, plus Lala's banjo. Her banjo's flight case looks exactly like a small coffin. A child's coffin, perhaps. It's so macabre that she taped a note to the outside that cheerfully proclaims, "Not a coffin."

This is a *lot* of luggage for me. I love minimalist travel, and when we planned our packing, there were times I longed to bring less. But Lala kept making the sensible point, "We are *moving countries*. Would you please accept the idea of checking baggage this one time?"

And she was right, of course. I brought a few things that I kept almost leaving out of my luggage, but now I'm so glad I didn't. They include:

1. My yoga mat. I haven't had a daily yoga practice in a long time, but it's coming back to me. And it feels good.

2. My lap desk. I bought it when I was sick earlier this

year and couldn't sit at my desk to write. It's great for working in bed, and it also has telescoping legs so that it can be used as a standing desk. It folds flat-ish but it's heavy and took up a lot of valuable real estate in my suitcase. I almost tossed it a hundred times. On the second day of being here, I used it to make the bathroom into a conference room while Lala took a call in the main room, and the desk suddenly justified every inch of space. In the last couple of days, I've taught classes standing in my little bathroom cubicle, I've filmed podcasts, I've been interviewed by a New Zealand book show, and I've appeared in an Instagram live with Cassie Roma, a host of *The Apprentice Aotearoa* (who is also quarantining in our hotel). From our *bathroom.*

3. Binoculars. I'm a very amateur birder, and yes, I've seen some new ones here. But you know what's *way* more interesting than birds when you're trapped in a hotel room? Watching the people down below in the parking lot walk around and around. With binoculars. #creeper #notsorry

4. Two fans, both USB-powered. One is a standing fan and has probably saved me from dying of spontaneous combustion during the night (the room is warm, the windows don't open, and the AC doesn't work). The fan folds down into a small, flat cylinder. And my folding USB fan that attaches to a battery bank and can also charge my Kindle and phone—invaluable.

5. Scrubba portable wash bag, size regular. I wasn't totally sure about this one, but I love it. It's basically a tough rubber bag that you put your laundry detergent into along with your clothes and water, and just like that, *squoosh-wash,* clean clothes. It has a little washboard built in! My new system: start the clothes soaking while I bathe, then washboard them in the bag while I'm still in the tub. Then I tumble the clothes into the bathwater where they get a

rinse. To dry, I wring them out, wrap them in a towel (and step on it), then hang the clothes on the travel clothesline. Lord, I love a system.

Day Seven

The phone rings. We've just woken up, and I stumble toward it, my first mug of tea in hand.

"Hello?" I'm expecting it to be housekeeping. Since they obviously can't come into our room, they call every few days to ask if we need more towels or toilet paper.

"Hello?" It's a man's voice, low and gravelly.

"Yes?"

"Hello?" he says again.

And just from those two words, I know who it is. "*Bill?*"

Bill is one of my students and a friend. He's a wonderful, sweet man who's writing his story of finding family (and himself) later in life. He's a delight.

And he's on the phone. With me. I don't think we've ever talked on the phone. Wait, I'm in New Zealand, and he's on the phone with me?

"Who's this?" he asks, obviously still thinking he's talking to reception.

"It's Rachael! Is this *Bill?*" But I know it is. Almost two decades of listening to short, chopped transmissions of 911 radio traffic have made me an expert at identifying people's voices from quick syllables.

Bill says he was trying to get the concierge service (this is not a concierge kind of hotel), and while explaining himself, they just transferred him to me.

Joy swims through me, quicksilver under my skin. I know, because of how kind he is, that he was probably trying to get the concierge so he could send me a present. I don't care about that, I'm just so thrilled at the sheer surprise of a *voice* that I adore coming out of nowhere. I don't think I've written the name of our hotel anywhere online—not out of caution, just because I haven't thought to do so.

"How did you *find* me?"

"Lala's tweet," he says. "That one with the picture of the volcano crater outside your hotel. I sent it to my son, and he looked at geo maps and figured out which place you were at."

My heart spins and chirps inside my chest. I didn't know I felt lost until I was found. Sure, this might have felt weird coming from a stranger. But Bill is part of my writing family. And what his call means is that Lala and I haven't gone so far that we can't be found, that we can't be supported and held.

We chat for a few more minutes. He says, "Love you," when we hang up and I say it back because it's true.

The next day, a basket full of live orchids and fancy New Zealand treats arrives at our door. I wear one of the orchids in my hair all day.

Day Ten

The thing I love best about this hotel? The bathtub.

It has two really big things going for it: first, its construction. Now, I'm not a small gal, and my belly rose above the level of an average overflow valve long ago. But unlike an American bath, there's no overflow valve at the top of this tub, which means you can fill it *all* the way up. There is a lip, maybe three quarters of an inch high, and this is magical: it means you can fill the tub and still scratch your nose without spilling water all over the floor.

The second-best thing about this tub?

When I'm in it, I'm not with Lala.

I'm alone.

Ten days into this adventure, we're in agreement on this one: we don't want to escape each other. This is a huge surprise to both of us. I'd honestly thought we might be sick to death of each other by now, but instead, we're still making each other laugh. We still have plenty to say to each other, all day long.

Yesterday, I said to her, "You know, it's so odd. I don't want to get away from you. I thought I would by now." We were sitting on our "picnic blanket," which is a towel we keep just for sitting on while we eat on the floor, because the desk is minuscule and usually covered with Lala's work computers.

"Well, that's good," she said, not looking up from her bite of lamb stew.

"But I sure *want to be alone.*"

She laughed, and I heard the relief in it. "Me fucking too."

And that's where the bath comes in handy. It's our alone time. I haven't taken baths this long since I had a claw-foot tub in my old condo, fifteen years ago. We're talking two-hour-long tubs. Two-and-a-half. I don't think I've hit the three-hour mark yet but that's only because our meals are delivered so regularly to our room that I usually have to get out and eat while the food is still hot.

Lala spends the same amount of time in there, so we're each getting at least four hours of alone time a day. I shudder to think what it would be like if we *didn't* have that tub.

Or if we didn't have this window, which I love. The wintery August sky is wide and dramatic, full of clouds that scud and bump and break, releasing rain that turns into mist and then rainbows. It doesn't really matter that we're looking down at ugly industrial buildings. It's enough to look up and *see* the Aotearoa sky.

Aotearoa, I whisper to myself, trying to correctly pronounce the te reo Māori name for this land.

Then I try to shrug off a soul discomfort that keeps itching at me the same way my skin does when I eat passionfruit.

I'm not sure I *deserve* to be here.

The border is closed. The only people who can cross it are New Zealanders and their families. Yes, I'm a New Zealand citizen, but I'm not really a Kiwi, like everyone else here. This a hotel full of people coming home. There are signs on all floors welcoming the "Returners." I'm not returning. I've never lived here before. Lala and I are both Americans, and though technically I'm also a New Zealander, I want with all my heart to be a Kiwi.

From up here on the sixth floor, I think about liminality every day. We look over the parking lot that's been converted to an exercise area. It's so small you can lap it in just a few minutes even if you're walking slowly. There's an outer walking ring, and an inner ring for the runners. I feel badly for them—it's a one-way flow, there's almost no part of their run that they're not banked in a turn. Their ankles must ache.

Twenty-five people are allowed outside at a time, and we have to be careful not to get too close to anyone else. The New Zealand Navy watch us closely as they guard New Zealand from us. They're very polite and interminably bored. Once I looked down and saw them hopping in the hopscotch zones the kids had drawn in chalk. I filmed their cheerful jumps and made it into a TikTok that went NZ-viral.

Tonight, as we reenter the hotel after our walk, the Navy guy at the door says, "Hey. You."

"*Me*?"

"You TikTok?"

I nod. Was that wrong? Will I get in trouble for filming the military? Oh, no, will they think I was making fun of them?

"That shit was funny, bro," he says.

I let out a breath of relief. "Was it you? Hopscotching?"

His gaze skitters sideways. "Yeah, nah. Not me. Some other guy."

Sure, dude. I see the joy of hopscotch in his eyes.

Day Thirteen

I don't want to leave.

God, that's so *stupid*. But I don't.

It's our last full day in the quarantine hotel. Sunday. A day off, ostensibly, but from what? I prowl around the hotel room, hunting for something to worry about. I snipe at Lala for not securing a walk time for us, even though I didn't ask her to. I worry that all the taxis in Auckland will be spoken for in the morning, and we won't be able to get one big enough to hold our luggage for the thirty-minute ride across town, to the rental where our New Zealand life will actually begin.

I get out my journal, and as I loop words up and down the pages, I get it. I figure out why I'm so fractious.

I write, *Change is scary as fuck*. Adding insult to injury, my favorite and last blue ballpoint pen runs out as I'm writing those exact words.

We've had nothing *but* change since the end of February when we started to do Moving Things.

But here? In this hotel? There's been no change. Absolutely none. There's been nothing to do but work, and read (I've finished seven books), and take baths, and sleep. Every meal is provided for us. We're safe and cozy. We want for nothing.

Tomorrow, everything will change.

We'll exit this liminal state and enter...

That's just it—I don't know what we'll enter.

When we look north out our hotel window, we can see the very tip-top of the Sky Tower. The place we're moving to tomorrow has an up-close view of the same tower, according to the pictures online.

So we're not moving far. I can almost see our next stop.

I should be able to slow my heart rate, shouldn't I? Why am I so scared?

It's not like our new life starts tomorrow. (*Yes, it does, yes, it does.*)

No. I reject that.

Our new life is here. Our new life is already *here.*

Already now. In this room.

As the thought moves through me, my heartbeat stills. Expands.

I get it. This is life too. It's all life. We haven't been waiting for anything. This has been a gorgeous interlude, a calm spot in which to rest after a few difficult years.

Maybe I'm *almost* ready to get out of here.

But there are still nine hours before bedtime, before our last sleep. I've already had a bath this morning, but there's time for another one after our two p.m. walk that Lala has talked them into letting us have. I can read at least another book today, can't I?

Tomorrow, it begins.
No, scratch that. That's not right.
Tomorrow, it *continues*.

Chapter 7

Stuck, with Bonus Birds

We're in the Bay of Islands, four hours north of Auckland, surrounded by greenery, water, and birds.

So many birds.

This morning, I hurry to lay out my yoga mat in the bedroom. It's seven o'clock. Lala got up to work about an hour ago—she's in the living room. My T-shirt and leggings aren't enough to keep me warm against the winter chill, but the yoga warms me up quickly. Then I meditate, desperately reaching for balance inside this unsettled time, but it's hard to concentrate on my breath. The coldness of the house sinks into my bones.

In the living room, I smell smoke, but the wood-burning stove is dark and cold. When I point this out to Lala, she scowls. "Yeah, you think? I've tried four times to light it. Keeps going out. Wood is wet."

In a classic opening-the-pickle-jar-because-someone-else-has-loosened-the-lid move, I relight the fire, coaxing it into warmth within a few minutes. "You must have dried it with your efforts."

"Hmph." Lala will never be accused of being a morning person.

I join her at the long wooden table in front of the fire. As I roll into doing my writing for the day, working on a book about novel-writing, I'd like to report that I go into full flow, diving deeply into the words.

But the birds are keeping me from writing.

To my left is a wall of glass that overlooks Te Wahapu Inlet. If I stand on the porch and throw a clamshell, I can hit the water. At high tide, the sea laps all the way up to the lawn. There's no road to the house—we can only get our car here at low tide, bumping along the shell-covered beach. If the tide's up, we leave the car in the parking lot a hundred yards down the beach.

The gleaming expanse of water is there as I write, its twinkling ripples always trying to snag my gaze. I'm working on a chapter about how to build an interesting secondary character when I see a flash of motion in my peripheral vision. Even as I plan to ignore it, my right hand has already reached for the binoculars.

It's a...pied cormorant? No, even better, it's a Caspian tern, the largest tern in the world! Its red bill and long white and black wings make it easily identifiable, and I watch with joy as it climbs into the rain then dives into the water in search of fish. It almost immediately bursts out of the water and back into the air—does that mean it swallowed its prey? Or did it come up empty-beaked? I can't tell.

What I do know is that I've lost track of what I was working on. Again.

I've never had such a view while writing. I've never worked—not to mention lived—in a house like this. We're currently just south of Russell, on a small inlet in the Bay of Islands. We meant to stay seven days, but we've been here a full month now because New Zealand went into full lockdown a week after we got out of our quarantine hotel, and we couldn't legally leave.

This was *not* the plan.

Last month, in Auckland, fresh out of quarantine, we did important life things, things that were harder than they sounded. In order to open a bank account, we needed a permanent address. But we didn't have one of those, so an acquaintance let us borrow her address, which had the effect of making me feel like a money launderer. Lying to a bank felt weird and wrong. And transferring money into that new bank account wasn't as easy as just writing a check —New Zealand doesn't do checks at all anymore, and besides, converting currencies in larger amounts than a couple of hundred dollars was complicated and expensive.

We got new phone plans and new phone numbers. We registered for our medical numbers, and I researched how to get a doctor to refill my normal medications. We got Inland Revenue Department numbers, then we filed for business IRD numbers too. All of these required lying about our "permanent" address, a house on the north shore of Auckland we've never been to.

By far the most difficult thing we did was buy a car. To buy a car, one must test drive that car, *on the left-hand side of the road,* in a city of a million and a half people. When I've driven in New Zealand in the past, I've always rented a car in the much less populated South Island before driving north, acclimating as I go. I've always ditched the rental before entering Auckland. I'm a good San Francisco driver —I know when to be aggressive and when to defer to other drivers. But driving in the big city on the wrong side of the road? I'm terrified. And Lala straight up won't do it, for which I don't blame her—at least I have experience, and she wants to take her time learning.

We go to a used car lot because it has a hybrid we'd like to view. I end up test-driving three cars, and I don't crash a single one. I'm relieved that the manager just looks at my US driver's license and hands me the keys. He doesn't come with us.

"A real money launderer would just steal this car," I say, trying to remain calm while figuring out how to navigate a busy roundabout.

Lala clutches her door handle. "He didn't even get a credit card to hold onto. *Whoa.*"

I've now gone round the roundabout twice. "I'm trying to get out!"

"Let's go back to the dealer!"

"Okay!" We're both shouting, but at least I'm back on the main street.

"Do you like how it drives?" Lala's voice is still too loud.

"I have no idea!" I'm just trying not to hit anything. Then we're back at the dealer, the windshield wipers flapping as I attempt and fail to signal my turn.

At a different dealership, the dealer rides with us in the car (perhaps he's smarter than the last guy). Because I'm trying to play it cool in front of him, I calm down enough to figure out that yes, I like this car. He gives us a great deal. Probably. Who knows? We sign the paperwork.

And then, a week after getting sprung from quarantine, we pack up our bags again and head north to Russell. Here, in this small seaside town, we'll spend our second week of freedom.

Really, we shouldn't even be in this house, which, at five hundred dollars a night in off-season (it's winter here now) is wildly outside our price range. I'd emailed the Airbnb host about his *other* property, the small, cheap one. I'd asked if it had good Wi-Fi because that's essential for both of our jobs. Dave wrote back, saying no, it was crap, but he had another house just sitting empty with strong Wi-Fi. The house had five bedrooms and was right on the water. He offered it to us for a hundred a night. It was still pretty pricey for us, but we took him up on it. When else would we get to stay in such a place with floor-to-ceiling windows facing the water?

Then New Zealand got a community case of Covid-19.

It's worth remembering New Zealand had stamped out the coronavirus. They'd had it when everyone else got it, at the beginning of 2020. They locked down tight for about eleven weeks, losing twenty-six people to it, and then there was no more coronavirus.

They'd *kept* it out by closing the borders to tourists (easy to do on an island) and setting up the MIQ hotels for citizens. Cases have popped up at those hotels, of course, but the infected were moved to total isolation and care, preventing Covid-19 from getting into the community.

So, for most of 2020 and 2021, New Zealand has operated normally. No masks. No Covid. After seventeen months of fear in the States, the first time Lala and I walked into a grocery store in Auckland with no masks on, I almost had a panic attack.

But then a case of Delta got into the community.

New Zealand locked down in mid-August, while we were still at this big, beachside house. Everything except hospitals and grocery stores closed. Travel of any sort was prohibited. Dave, our host, grateful to have any guests at all, allowed us to stay at the same low rate.

And I'll admit this: there was a small part of me that was *thrilled*. I hated the circumstances, of course. I'd much rather not be locked down. But the apartment we'd rented in Auckland had been dark and depressing, with windows surrounded by taller buildings. Natural light never made its way inside. What if we'd been trapped *there,* in a dark high-rise? Instead, we were here, on the bay, the water lapping at our literal doorstep. How long could we get away with pretending this was our home?

I had birds to watch, after all.

When the coronavirus first broke out in the States, my sister gave me the book, *How to Do Nothing,* by Jenny Odell. I was freaked out by the idea of actually doing *nothing,* but the book got me interested in birdwatching, which Odell learned to do while trying to do less.

I ordered a bird feeder and put it up right outside my office window. I became friendly with the chickadees and goldfinches. But aside from a red-shouldered hawk who nested in our backyard eucalyptus, there weren't any *exciting* birds in our part of Oakland.

That's not the case here. Oh, no.

I love the white-faced heron's smooth flight, and I adore the variable oystercatchers with their orange eyes and long carrot noses. The first time I saw an eastern rosella, I couldn't believe what I was seeing—was it a tiny parrot? Wearing a leopard-print coat? Right in front of me?

But the tūī has won my heart.

Go ahead, google "tūī song." You won't regret it. Above their little white cravats, they open their mouths and emit loud R2D2 noises. A couple of them around here sing the *Hallelujah* part of Handel's *Messiah* (seriously, one must have learned those four notes then taught the others in the area) before switching into metallic chirps and whistles.

Lala is obsessed with their sound, but what I enjoy best is the way they fly.

Tūī fly like they got the flight manual but never bothered to read it, shamelessly hurling themselves into the air, their wings flapping so mightily that you can identify them just by the *buzz-buzz* of their wings. There's nothing subtle about them. And when they're going fast, they just kind of stop flying, pinning their wings against their bodies, so it looks as if they've been shot from a tiny invisible cannon. Then they fall earthward, chirping a beat or two of trip-hop before catching themselves. Again, they hurtle upward with a great wind rush of flapping, then glide a few more yards before falling, drunken circus clowns of the air.

Whether or not we're watching the tūī, their electronic chitter is the background to everything we do. On that first day of lockdown, Lala and I sat side by side in front of my computer to watch the first address by the prime minister. The tūī chirped away while she spoke.

Without apology, Jacinda Ardern said we were locking down to save New Zealand. (The vaccine has only rolled out here in the last few weeks—NZ is the one of the last developed nations to gain access to it, with only five percent of its population vaccinated so far.)

She took questions from reporters, calling on them by name, answering each one frankly, with consideration and knowledge. She was like the calmest, most well-informed press secretary you've ever seen, except she was *also the big boss*. She threw the scientific questions to Dr. Ashley Bloomfield, New Zealand's Director-General of Health, who answered questions just as clearly.

I watched two people speak who stood for the country we now live in. They were truthful. *And* kind.

My throat tightened. Pain bloomed behind my eyes. My fingers started shaking.

I didn't *understand*. Why was I so upset? I felt safe. I'm vaccinated, and hell, I lived through seventeen months of Covid-19 in the States, most of those months without a vaccine. I have an autoimmune disease and am immuno-compromised, but I believe in science. I know if I get the virus, the chances are excellent that it will be a mild case, and if it isn't, I'll get good care.

But my body was screaming at me. I stopped listening to Jacinda so I could listen to what was going on inside my skin.

Grief. Anger. A one-two punch that almost doubled me over.

Here were the adults in the room. They were taking care of us.

Over the top of my computer, I watched two wood pigeons jostle for the right to sit on a tree branch. Their bodies blurred as I lost the fight to keep back my tears.

Lala's face was drawn, her eyes tight. When she spoke, it was through gritted teeth. "It could have been so different."

As the lockdown continues, every day at one p.m., Jacinda and Ashley get up in front of the nation and give scientific facts, relay the new stats, and answer every question.

Their knowledge and compassion remain impressive, but I've stopped watching the daily briefing, picking up its key points on the New Zealand Twitter account. Oh, how quickly I've adjusted to being taken care of.

The bird watching is enough to keep my attention. Not to brag, but if you open the eBird app and go to the Far North District of New Zealand, you will see that Rachael Herron is, at the time of writing, thirty-sixth of the top hundred eBirders, with twenty-two species spotted. I *know*! What a freakin' *legend*. I check that rank more than I check social media.

It's not what we envisioned we'd be doing now. We did, after all, move to New Zealand to be adventurous. To scout a different city every week. To explore. To be *unstuck*, carrying with us only our suitcases, hopes, and dreams.

We are, one could argue, pretty damn stuck now.

There's nothing within walking distance, and we're not supposed to drive unless we need food or a doctor. We're not supposed to kayak (because if we got into trouble, we'd be putting first responders at potential Covid-19 risk to rescue us) so I do my best to ignore how shiny and red the kayaks are in the driveway.

But we still walk every day, normally separately, to get alone time. I go up the road about a mile and come back down. There's no traffic, obviously, which is good, because there are also no sidewalks. I walk in the middle of the road, watching sacred kingfishers cling to phone lines. The bay stretches around me on both sides of the narrow spit of land, and I watch clouds cast shadows on the water lapping against the sand. The empty boats bob on their moorings, as abandoned as the kayaks.

I work. I've written half a book and am teaching a new crop of classes.

And in my downtime, I sit on the porch with a cup of tea, binoculars in my lap. It's a pleasing juggling act—pushing down my glasses and raising binoculars to my eyes all while keeping the bird-identifying app close at hand.

White wings, black tips. Wait, black wings, white tips? Thank god I didn't leave the binoculars behind because they took up too much room in my suitcase, something I considered at least ten times. Now I keep them in close reach and use them all day long.

As I type this, the tide is high. An hour ago, we decided to get groceries in town. But then we realized that the car is in the driveway and we can't drive out until low tide, so we sat back down again.

Sitting wasn't what we had planned for this month. We got out of quarantine with every intention of doing as little sitting as humanly possible.

Turns out, the plan was different. Turns out, the plan would involve sitting, and binoculars, and birds, and feeling safe.

Rumor has it lockdown will ease this week. Soon, we'll get into the car and drive away from this house we've been in for a month. I do worry that I've been spoiled for every other place I'll ever live. How am I supposed to go back to staying in apartments with windows that look out at cars and walls, not an ever-changing body of water and birds of many colors?

A month of memories: walking through the rain on the quiet road. Admiring the carrot-nosed oystercatchers and their silly walk. Spying a weka's chicken-duck stride running through the front yard. Building the fire in the living room and stoking it, over and over.

But my favorite memory from this place is from an evening when it *poured* down onto the tin roof, a cacophony of thundering water. Night had just fallen, the sunset only a brief glow, quickly extinguished. I put chicken and sliced kumara (sweet potato) into the oven and left them to roast. The fire roared in the wood stove. I carried a mug of tea doctored with creamy milk and a touch of manuka honey out to the table on the front porch. Just like all the other nights, I sat out there with my mug and the binoculars, and I didn't come inside until I'd finished the tea. I didn't read. I didn't look at my phone unless it was to identify a bird. I just breathed and watched the dark water move.

That stormy night, I couldn't see any birds, of course, but through the sound of the downpour, every once in a while I heard a single tūī chirp, singing the beginning of its *hallelujah* as if surprised to find itself still there, still safe, in the rain.

Chapter 8

Behind the Scenes

Instagram photo:

A waterfall crashes into a blue-green lagoon, the curtain of water sending up a rush of white spray. The surrounding landscape is green and lush, suggesting we've hiked (or as Kiwis say, tramped) through the bush for miles to reach this secluded, idyllic place.

Behind the scenes:

It's almost impossible to take a picture of Whangarei Falls without also taking a picture of the parking lot above it. Disappointment blooms in my chest, itchy like poison oak.

We've pulled over because the sign on the highway told us to, and because I have to pee. I expected the falls to be at least a *bit* of a hike, but it turns out these falls are just steps away from a retirement home and—thank goodness—a public toilet.

We take the requisite photos and use the bathroom. We get back on the road, our new-to-us car packed full. The hybrid Toyota station wagon looks and handles like a compact, but it's a veritable Tardis, holding way more than it looks like it could.

And that's good. In addition to our four suitcases, four backpacks, and the banjo coffin, now we have eleventy-million kitchen bags. While in lockdown in Russell, we cooked every meal at our Airbnb home, so we now have a traveling pantry full of groceries and essentials (fish sauce and olive oil and balsamic vinegar and sweet chili sauce and all the spices we routinely use).

I feel the full weight of the car as I negotiate keeping it on the left-hand side of the road.

"You're *kind* of on the edge over here." Lala's voice is strangled.

"Damn it. Thanks." I'm getting better at driving here, but I still stray too close to the margin of the road when logging trucks blow past in the opposite direction on the two-lane motorway.

My hands tighten harder on the wheel the closer we get to Auckland. Our goal is to drive south through the city to Mount Maunganui, a beach town seven hours from Russell.

That goal is made harder because we're not *totally* sure what we're doing is legal.

Aotearoa has gone into a softer lockdown. Everything has opened up with mandatory mask use indoors.

Except for Auckland. They're still getting case after case of Covid-19, so the borders of the city are shut tight, guarded by police. Aucklanders are allowed one walk a day in their neighborhoods, but otherwise, they have to stay inside, hunkered down.

We are north of Auckland, and we need to be south of it.

Technically, if you have a government-ordered reason to

move *through* Auckland without stopping, you can do it. Those reasons include things like emergencies, funerals, and going back home if you've been trapped in lockdown away from it. But we don't have a home. Does moving from one Airbnb to another count? Last week, I'd prowled the internet but couldn't find a clear answer. Moving for vacation reasons? Totally out of the question. Relocating? Allowed if you were moving to a permanent home. What we were doing? A gray area.

Finally, I asked the NZ government at their Twitter account (oh, yes, I did) if we could legally move through Auckland.

They said yes. Had I perhaps confused an intern? Were they just in a good mood?

Didn't matter. I took a screenshot of their answer, we packed our bags, and now we're on the road.

At the northern Auckland border, I hold out my phone to the policeman. "We have permission to cross through." I pray my Twitter screenshot looks more official to him than it does to me.

His eyebrows draw together and his voice is baffled. "Um, let me check a few things."

My hands sweat. Lala says something, but I barely hear her. *We're not going to get through the barricade, and we have no other place to stay—we'll lose the money we've had to prepay on the next week's Airbnb, and that'll blow the budget...* Even though my window is still open and it can't be more than fifty degrees outside, sweat drips down the side of my face. I crank the AC.

He comes back. "You can pass through. But if they ask you on the other side, make sure you tell them that where you're going is your new home, and this is a permanent relocation. We've tagged your plate—you know you can't stop, right? Do not stop. Not to get fuel. Not even to use the bathroom."

I nod and take off before he changes his mind.

"That felt close," says Lala.

My neck is made of knots, the pain rising into the base of my skull. But relief feels like clear, sweet water. "We did it. Now we just have to get out."

And that's when it hits me.

Oh, shit.

I've been so worried about getting *into* the Auckland area that I'd forgotten to worry about getting out. I'm an idiot. Getting out will be the hard part. Who really cares if people enter the danger zone? That's on them. Most police efforts will focus on preventing the disease from getting out by keeping people *in*. Obviously.

That cop hadn't guaranteed us exit. He'd just told us what to say to up our chances.

"What if we can't get past the border?"

"That's the worry, yes." Lala has already figured that out.

Driving through the closed region is supposed to take about an hour and a half, going at the 100 kph speed limit. I keep my eye on the speedometer, determined to hit the border at exactly the time they'll be looking for our license plate.

Then Google Maps loses the plot, the disembodied voice telling me that the road is closed ahead. She says to get off the highway and take winding back roads, which I do for a while. But I have a good sense of direction, and I know it isn't right. I put us back on the highway.

Google Maps takes me off it again.

It isn't until I've battled the woman in my phone for at least twenty minutes before I realize what she's doing: *she is trying to route us around the roadblocks.* To her, they look like wasted time.

To the cops on the other side, it will look like we've stopped along the way.

I get back on the motorway and hit the gas, doing 110, then 120 kph. Better to get a speeding ticket than to be stuck for the unknowable future in a city we don't want to live in.

At the border, I'm in a flop-sweat again, panting. My Twitter story seems less believable this time, but the cop here is young and green.

"You're *moving,*" he clarifies, peering into the back of the car. "Yes?"

It's not a coffin.

"Yes," I say firmly. "Our new home is in Mount Maunganui." It's not quite the truth, but it's also not quite a lie.

Finally, after a whispered conversation with two other officers, he waves us through.

The migraine grows behind my eyes, and we still have three hours to drive. We celebrate our escape by sharing a gas station meat pie, and I swallow the exhaustion and pain along with the mince.

Instagram photo:

Lala sits at a picnic table at her laptop, the grass bright green, the sky bright blue. To her left, a puppy bounds into the picture, and on her other side stand two cows, placidly chewing their cud. Caption: *Lala's new office.*

. . .

Behind the scenes:

We are sleeping in a shed.

On the other side of the living room wall is where the owners of this small farm keep their equipment. While I load the tiny dishwasher, I hear them moving buckets and tools.

They've done up the space nicely, and I have to admit it's warm and cozy. The tiny kitchen has everything you'd need, including fresh bread and homemade jams.

But it's *small.*

It's honeymoon sized. It's two-steps-to-cross-the-room small. Since leaving Russell six weeks ago, we've been moving town to town every seven days, and I'm *tired.* So we've rented this place for ten days, but I preemptively regret nine of them as soon as we enter the space. The mid-century couch is the most uncomfortable thing I've ever sat on, and the only restful piece of furniture is the bed. The single table is small enough that you can caress your beloved's cheek at any moment, except that Lala and I both have to work full time with back-to-back meetings that the internet is too slow to support.

As my classes are currently in session, I need reliable Wi-Fi, so I find a coworking spot a fifteen-minute drive away in the closest one-horse town. I rent the only private room and position my computer so that a black wall is behind me, making my silver hair appear startlingly bright. On screen, I think my image looks kind of cool, but what my students and podcast guests can't see is that the other walls are made of crookedly hung plywood. Whenever I plug in my computer, a blue spark leaps. The plug falls out of the socket, over and over, the spark crackling every time. The sliding door to the room is stuck on its runners and doesn't close all the way, so I feel like an asshole, talking constantly, my voice filtering out to the main room where other people work in the shared space. They chat and gossip with each other, clearly friends. I'm the interloper. I try to smile in a friendly manner, but the smile feels fake, and no one makes eye contact with me.

Next door is a cafe where I get the best cheese scone I've ever had (toasted, butter dripping from every surface). I resolve to eat one daily while I'm here. The barista asks my name for my drink, and on my second visit, she calls me Rachael. I want to ugly-cry with gratitude. Her name is Annie, and in my imagination, we become best friends. She looks forward to seeing me every day—she knows my order and gives me a secret discount while chatting with me about her kids and the painting she's working on. Her mom's doing well with the chemo, and her sister's coming to town next week, can I come for dinner?

In reality, Annie just smiles at me, and five days into our relationship, she writes Rochelle on my takeaway cup.

When I get back to the shed from the office, the space is still too small even though I've been out of it all day. Lala is my favorite person, but Jesus Christ, we see enough of each other. So I go for long solo walks. If I circumnavigate the surrounding fields, going around the "block" and turning right every time I come to a road, I can make it all the way back to the shed in about an hour. There are no sidewalks, so I walk in the road. It doesn't matter—there's almost no traffic, and when drivers see me, they move over to the wrong side of the road to make sure I know they won't hit me. Almost all of them wave as they pass. I wave back wildly, feeling like I'm giving the "I'm drowning" gesture.

If only one of the cars would stop for a bit of a chat.

Maybe I could carry a hand-lettered sign. *I would like to be friends. I am not a serial killer.*

Then again, there's a bench in town that has a mural behind it that reads: *Happy to Chat: Sit here if you don't mind someone stopping to say hello.*

I keep a *very* close eye on that bench. If someone sat on it while I was looking, I would beeline my way there to say that hello and grab that chat.

But I can't make myself sit on the bench alone. The whole town would know I wasn't local, and they'd know what the bench was for, and they'd walk by without meeting my eyes, and my heart would fall out of my chest and pump the last of its blood into the gutter.

One afternoon, while on my long walk around the block, I hear bleating. That's not rare—I've heard a lot of baaing as I walk past fields full of new, muddy lambs and confused-looking mamas. But this sounds different—it sounds like multiple lambs are insistently demanding something. I imagine for a moment that they're calling for me, then, as I see them, I realize they *are.*

Normal lambs run away across the paddock if you step even an inch closer to them. These two aren't normal lambs. They love people—perhaps they're orphans being raised by hand. Both are wearing collars, and they race to the fence line to greet me. I crash to my knees in the muddy grass, reaching through the wire to scratch the spot just behind their ears. I talk to them, and they talk back, and it doesn't matter that we don't speak the same language—when I reluctantly leave them to finish my walk, we are friends.

They're never in that paddock again.

. . .

Instagram photo:

Lala and Rachael stand in front of a steep hill (that they've earlier climbed to the top of, thank you very much) while a sunset blazes over the turquoise ocean water. Both are grinning.

Behind the scenes:

We're staying in an adorable beach town. The shops along the main road remind me of the California beach town I grew up in—saltwater taffy and hamburger stands and gift shops selling multicolored prints of seagulls dodging neon-colored waves.

The problem is that it's not beach season. Winter has just rolled over to spring, and the rain is near constant. Even if it were beach season, the town is obviously set up for parties: large groups of family and friends who congregate to kitesurf and boogie board and scuba dive.

If it were summer, it would still be just Lala and me.

No family.

No friends.

Just the two of us.

From the minuscule apartment in this beach town, I send video messages to my loved ones. It's not a live back-and-forth conversation—it's like texting, but with video, which they watch at their leisure with no need to worry about time zones. I start each message cheerfully and end apologizing for the crying that roars over me like the squalls that gust outside the windows.

The rain continues for days, lashing the cranes and container ships visible out the sliding glass door. Everything is a deep, sodden gray. My weather app sugarcoats nothing, saying tomorrow will again be *Dreary*.

Next to the cranes is a huge pile of white salt, a whole mountain of it. In the middle of the night, Lala grabs me out of a sound sleep. "Why doesn't the salt dissolve in the rain?"

Together, we silently stare up at the ceiling, wondering. Light bleeds around the shade of the window that inexplicably faces the apartment building's shared hallway.

Why *doesn't* the salt dissolve?

(We google the answer the next morning, and it has to do with the chemical bonding of wet salt. It's not crystals of salt—the top layer is a big *chunk* of salt, like an enormous salt lick in the shape of a mountain. The non-magical explanation deflates me.)

Things look up when Wendy Vella, a local writer, meets me for coffee, and unable to stop myself, I turn into a golden retriever. I bounce. I grin. I do everything but lick her face. I try to keep the desperate happiness out of my voice, but it's impossible. We talk about the business of writing for two hours, nonstop, until the cafe closes. My heart sings as I walk back to the apartment. *A real friend.* My first Kiwi friend, made on my own terms, not those of proximity (read: the Airbnb hosts who have to talk to us).

Back in the apartment, I flatten again. Being with a new person was amazing, but I won't hang out with Wendy anytime soon. We're moving again in a few days.

Photo *not* posted on Instagram:

My red face as Lala nixes my next choice of Airbnb home for looking too boring. "Fine!" I push the computer away from me. "*You* pick a place." I grab my phone clumsily, and as usual, it takes a picture I'm not prepared for, showing me my own furious scowl.

. . .

Behind the scenes:

Our goal has been to spend a week in places we think we might want to live, working Tuesday through Saturday (American workdays, since Lala works for a US-based company), moving on Sunday, and exploring on Monday. Repeat, and repeat again. Airbnbs are plentiful, and since there are still no tourists in New Zealand, we're doing the economy and the hosts a favor.

But finding rentals with all four things we want is hard. 1) Heat. I promised Lala she'd be warm. Some kind of heater in the house is essential for us, but not for hardy Kiwis, who take pride in going barefoot and wearing shorts in the dead of winter. 2) Fast Wi-Fi. We've found that some places that say they have strong Wi-Fi actually have dial-up speed that flickers in and out as the wind gusts. 3) A table big enough for two people to work and eat at. Surprisingly, many rentals don't have a table at all, just barstools at a counter. 4) Laundry: this is only a nice-to-have. We could, after all, go to a laundromat. But this turns out to be the easiest amenity to find. Almost every place we stay has a washer and dryer. I suppose in the dead of winter you can wrap a blanket hot out of the dryer around your body to make up for the fact that the apartment you booked is fifty-six degrees Fahrenheit inside, but I'd rather have a heater.

Picking a new place every week is exhausting. Even deciding on a *town* is difficult. But how will we figure out where to live if we don't visit every place? Nelson is gorgeous (we'd had a great meal there seven years before) but would it be too small for us? Auckland—it's just *too* big, isn't it? We love Wellington, but isn't it too pricey? We're heading vaguely for the more affordable Christchurch area, but on the way, shouldn't we spend a week in every likely area? New Plymouth? Napier? Dunedin?

If we visit each town, feel them all out, feed them through our columns of plusses and minuses, we'll be able to make a completely informed decision about where to put down our ripped-up roots.

Lala stares at her iPad, stabbing at it. She pushes it at me and I look at her Airbnb suggestion.

"No Wi-Fi," I say.

The triumph I feel is the equivalent of marital heartburn.

Instagram Photo:

A sunset shot of a log on the beach, the clouds lit with orange and yellow rays as if heaven is pouring out buckets of light. Photo taken on our way to the hot pools because cameras aren't allowed inside the spa.

Behind the scenes:

At the outdoor spa, family and friends gather to gossip and play. Couples canoodle, and kids jump into the shallow areas wearing water wings. There are five or six gigantic pools, all different temperatures, with plenty of room in each one. The early spring air is chilly, so the hot water feels incredible, especially since it's been a while since we stayed in a place with a bathtub.

Lala and I read our Kindles. We're the only ones reading, but hey, we talk to each other all day, every day. Now is for reading, for carefully holding our devices out of the water and getting lost in the words.

I'm reading a book that's blowing my mind: *Four Thou-*

sand Weeks by Oliver Burkeman. Ostensibly a time management book (which is eternally my catnip), he posits that we'll never have time to do everything we want to do, so we should accept that fact, and give up trying. We don't have to throw out the To-Do lists, but we must face the difficult truth that our lives are short and failure to check all the boxes is inevitable. As I read, I feel both called out and well-loved at the same time.

He says that because life is so short, you should decide in advance what you'll fail at. Then, when you let the lawn get overrun with Bermuda grass, you won't feel as bad, because you'd already decided that the lawn was less important than, say, writing your novel or hanging out with your kids.

A boy skids past me on the wet tile. I only glance up for a second before dropping my gaze again. Burkeman is writing about people who try to fit everything into their lives. People like me.

"This helps explain why stuffing your life with pleasurable activities so often proves less satisfying than you'd expect. It's an attempt to devour the experiences the world has to offer, to feel like you've truly lived—but the world has an effectively infinite number of experiences to offer, so getting a handful of them under your belt brings you no closer to a sense of having feasted on life's possibilities. Instead, you find yourself pitched straight back into the efficiency trap. The more wonderful experiences you succeed in having, the more additional wonderful experiences you start to feel you could have, or ought to have, on top of all those you've already had, with the result that the feeling of existential overwhelm gets worse."

Holy shit.

I've been trying to see *all* the cities in New Zealand

before we decide where to settle down. I've been trying to work out the *best* choice, to figure out the one right answer.

That's impossible.

We can't do it.

The relief is so enormous that my brain feels filled with helium, and I might just float up into the sky.

We don't even have to try.

I tap Lala on the shoulder. "We can't visit every city in New Zealand before we decide where to live."

She lowers her reading glasses. "I know that."

"Why didn't you *tell* me?"

Her eyes widen. "Did you really think we could?"

I take a moment to look up into the night sky overhead. "No."

She *hmmms*.

"Okay, maybe I thought we could."

"Of course you did." Her voice is as warm as the water.

"So what should we do?" I ask.

"Stop moving every single week?"

More relief floods through me. It's been harder and harder to get up early and pack everything and load the car every week. I nod. "Yeah."

"And maybe go check out that house in Wellington, for real?" Lala had seen a post in a Facebook group about a young couple who were moving from New Zealand to the US and needed the lease of their flat taken over.

I wipe water droplets off my face and say, "We do love Wellington." Seven years before, Lala had stood with me on the edge of the glittering harbor. *I want to live here,* she'd said. It's an incredibly expensive city to live in and the rental market is difficult.

Lala says, "We do."

I think about the Ellen Langer quote: *Don't make the*

right decision; make the decision right. "It doesn't matter, does it? We just choose and then work with that."

She slides her glasses back up her nose and nods.

We both go back to reading.

In my heart, I know we're heading to Wellington.

Chapter 9

Moon, Upside Down

Lala says, "Hey!" She's working at the breakfast bar. "That Wellington couple got back to us."

We thought this most recent Airbnb had a table when we rented it. It doesn't. I'm on the couch, practicing poor ergonomics, balancing my laptop on my knees. "Yeah?"

"Look."

I get up and peek over Lala's shoulder. "Those pictures can't be real."

"You never know."

Lala scrolls through photos of the harbor, sailboats dotted on the blue water. "They say they'll do a virtual tour with us today if we want to."

I groan. I *don't* want to. I'm fighting a migraine and losing. I predict I have about four more hours of brain-time before it fully lands and I have to knock myself out with drugs to sleep through the pain. I don't want to waste time meeting strangers online to do a virtual tour of a house we'll never live in. Have I mentioned that one of my migraine symptoms is irritability?

"Even if we love it, we probably wouldn't get it. You know the rental market in Wellington." I say this as if either of us knows anything more than what we've read on the internet.

"It can't hurt."

I rub at my eyelids, trying to push away the pain and a low rumble of unease that takes me a minute to identify. "But...wouldn't it...wouldn't it be too easy? Too fast? If we take over their lease...when did they say? November? We'll have been traveling for less than six months. What about our dreams of seeing more cities? Of digital nomading for at least a year?"

"I thought you said you were cool with choosing something. With *not* seeing every city in the country. What happened to that Rachael?"

"That Rachael sounds like an idiot."

Lala says, "I think we should look at it."

"Fine," I snap. "*You* look at it and tell me what you think."

But when the time to meet them on Zoom rolls around, I've gotten even grumpier, which means I don't want Lala to see the apartment without me. I drag myself to the barstool next to her and fold my arms, preparing to hate everything they show us.

Please file this under *Duh*: I do not hate everything.

By the time we hang up with Cassidy and Sam, I want to live in their apartment. It's more like a house, the whole upper half of a 1930s villa on the side of a hill. The only other person who lives in the house is a professor in the downstairs unit, and apparently he's very quiet. Cassidy and Sam hold their computer up to the windows and dangle it off the balcony, showing us breathtaking 180-degree views of the Wellington harbor.

"I told you so," says Lala.

I don't even mind. I just say, "I was wrong. You were right. You were totally right. Want to apply for it tonight?"

She stares, obviously wondering if she should call me an ambulance.

It turns out I *hate* being a digital nomad.

What a pretentious term it is. The bro-ness of it makes me shudder. I picture single young men living in Bali, carrying around a backpack that holds their laptop and one change of clothes. Body odor is caked into their travel T-shirts, but they don't think they smell because, hey, this shirt cost a hundred bucks and it's *merino*. They date local women they fetishize, and in their heart of hearts, they can't wait to get their start-up funded so they can buy a condo in San Francisco.

Of course, *I* would do it differently. My Rachael the Digital Nomad fantasy looks similar, but oh, so different. My only piece of luggage is also a backpack, and yes, it holds my laptop, but it also holds my journal because I'm more *sensitive* than they are. I carry *two* changes of clothes because I don't stink. I wash the day's clothing every night and dry it the next day, even if my lightweight blue travel dress has to hang fetchingly from my bag as I dash to catch the next train, smiling at the porter who's obviously wondering where this fascinating young woman is off to next.

Obviously, in this fantasy, I'm young and single. I'm closer to being called "miss" than the real-life late-forties "ma'am." There's no room in that small backpack for a CPAP, and that's okay. *Sleep apnea? Never heard of her*.

In real life, as we move around New Zealand, I realize

that no part of what we've been doing matches any nomadic fantasy I've ever had. We are *not* traveling light and fast, like glimmering dragonflies. We're ponderous water bugs, laboriously lumbering from place to place, swearing at our suitcases and snapping at each other because our backs hurt from lifting them into the back of the car.

In every Airbnb, I unpack. I am, after all, the queen of packing and unpacking, and it usually gives me great pleasure. But three or four Airbnbs later, I start losing even *that* joy.

In our current place, I've left my clothes in the suitcase. The apartment is the size of a dollhouse, so I don't have much choice, but I don't fight it either. I'm giving up. And I'm too tired to care.

We apply to take over the lease of the Wellington flat.

Cassidy and Sam like us, so they're not showing the apartment to anyone else. We're the only ones they present to their landlord for approval of transferring the lease.

We're still three hours north of Wellington when the landlord's approval comes through.

Holy cow. In six weeks, we'll have a home again.

The next time I lift my suitcases into the back of the car, they do not feel *light* exactly, but they certainly don't weigh me down the same way. "I'm unpacking you soon," I promise my bags. "Oh, how I will unpack you."

Cassidy and Sam are moving to the States to be with Cassidy's family, and in a fortuitous turn of events, they need to sell everything they own. Oh, hey! It turns out that we need to buy almost everything! Our boxes of stuff will eventually arrive, but they're mostly full of books, clothing, and memorabilia. We need *things*.

Sam makes a detailed spreadsheet of everything they own, what they paid for it, and their asking price. Then they knock an additional thirty percent off the total. There are fifty steps up to the flat, and they're just grateful they don't have to carry anything down. "Tell us what you want, and we'll leave it for you."

Yes, we want the Crock-Pot and the air fryer and the KitchenAid and the printer (all of which use the correct New Zealand voltage, unlike the ones we got rid of in the States). We will absolutely take the dishes and the towels and the big couch and the two beds. Yes, we want the barbecue and the outdoor furniture and the ottoman and the games stored in that ottoman. Yes, we totally want the TV and the modem and the two desks and the spare monitor.

"We'll take it all."

Sam gives me his bank account number, and I transfer the funds from our account to his (because that's how Kiwis do it), adding twenty percent back on out of sheer gratitude that we are furnishing an entire house—this whole *life*—for just a few thousand dollars.

Six weeks later, we move in.

Cassidy and Sam have left the key (our key!) under the mat. We open the door with a twist and a little shove (the door sticks in the humidity), and we're inside. This place is *ours*.

In the dining room, we stand and stare, our arms around each other.

Morning sun breaks over the harbor, gleaming so brightly it almost hurts to look at. Below us on the hill are houses (such lovely, sweet, traditional wood-framed houses) and so many trees. At the base of the hill, a passenger train rattles past, followed shortly by a freight train pulling adorable half-sized containers. Just past the rails runs the motorway—morning traffic streams at a steady pace into the capital city. Just past *that,* cars and trucks load onto the Interislander ferry, as big as a cruise liner, roaring companionably in place. Above the ferry, a plane descends, prepping to land at Wellington International.

"Planes, trains, and automobiles," I say.

"One of us had to say it."

"Let's unpack!" For nine months, since February, all I've done is either get rid of things or cart the remaining things around with me in those wretched suitcases. I'm going to *put things away.*

But first, I explore.

We've just purchased a glorious grab bag of stuff, sight unseen, and I'm dying to know what we own. It's kind of like—no, it is *exactly* like moving into an Airbnb, except we don't have to leave and we own everything in it.

I pull open a drawer in the kitchen. Oooh, we own string, the kind with which you tie up a chicken! Having a ball of twine in the kitchen drawer is a very grown-up thing to have, and my chest puffs immediately with pride that I have just become that kind of grown-up.

The cutlery is heavy and nice, nicer than ours, and I regret that somewhere in a box on its way to us is a hodgepodge of mismatched cutlery we've acquired over the years without conscious decision. Our new bowls are plain white, a choice we never would have made, but their sturdy heft is pleasing.

The towels in the bathroom—none of them are stained, not even one. They're fluffy and they match. Those twenty-somethings, man. They know how to *live.*

They also, bless them, appear to have taken us at our word when I said, *We'll take it all.*

It's my fault—I'd been very clear with them. *If you don't want to take something with you, just leave it. We'll get rid of anything we don't want.* We even ran into them at the museum yesterday. They were meeting friends, and I thought they looked suspiciously relaxed for people who were going to move out of the country the next day.

Now I know why they were relaxed. They packed their suitcases and left the rest.

The pantry is still full of their half-eaten food. The fridge holds open bags of lettuce and almost-empty condiment jars. The bathroom cabinets are stuffed with toiletries and hair products, razors and shaving cream. In the drawers I find underwear, old T-shirts, and expired prescriptions.

I feel a sharp twinge of trash day PTSD. In Oakland, once our trash can was full, we were screwed until the next week rolled around. Our small can held two full kitchen bags, *maybe* three if you really pounded them in. For months, as we'd packed and readied to move, every Monday I'd done an early morning walk of shame through the neighborhood, peeking into the cans set on the curb, hoping for space to sneakily dump our extra trash.

Taking a deep breath, I remember that it's better here. Trash pickup is genius. You don't pay monthly. Instead, you buy big yellow city council bags from the grocery store. They're $3.10 each, and boom—you've just paid for trash service. Recycling goes into big clear bags, which are free, and this motivates you to recycle as much as possible. On trash day, you can put out as many of each kind of bag as you want. You just set out the bags on the street the night before your collection day. No trash cans. Since there are neither squirrels nor raccoons in New Zealand, nothing rips open the bags, which we find miraculous.

So, on the day we move in, I spin into Tasmanian devil mode, filling bag after bag with trash. I put stuff that isn't trash but that we don't want aside to take to the thrift stores, and unpack our own things into the newly empty spaces.

As my suitcases empty, my heart gets lighter and lighter.

Then it's time to choose our offices.

One whole side of the house faces the harbor, so the kitchen, the dining room, the master bedroom, and the living room all feature the jaw-dropping water views. Sam and Cassidy had slept in the master bedroom. But either the bed needs to be put with its head against the window, which means we wouldn't see the view at all, or it would be against a wall where only one person could see the water from bed, and only awkwardly, at that. Plus, the room faces east, and we know it'll get hot and bright early in the day. Not an ideal sleeping room. Lala, however, loves hot and bright. Her office it becomes. I'm only the tiniest bit jealous of her view.

I take Cassidy's old office for my own. It faces the garden, all green grass and trees. There's a small, raised garden bed slanting up the hill, and I plan to put things into the ground immediately.

The last bedroom, the tiny one, was Sam's office. It's dark and small and faces a concrete retaining wall. If you stand right against the window, you can peer up the green hill and into the trees, but it's not a room with a view. We make it our bedroom. To get to it, you have to spiral through the house, around the bathroom, through the dining room, curling through the middle hallway, and then finally, into the room. Somehow, walking that sleepy spiral makes the room feel impossibly cozy and safe. There's room—just barely—for the queen-sized bed, and I have to turn sideways to get to my side of it, but it's such a good, quiet bedroom.

Lala and I are home.

We are *home*—the single syllable is a glorious song stuck in my head. Home, home, *home*.

That first night, I'm exhausted but not ready to go to bed just yet. I make a cup of tea and carry it onto the deck to watch the clouds scud over the harbor. At eight forty-five, the sunset flares behind me, sending pinks and purples eastward, toward the mountains we face on the other side of the water. At the same time, the Interislander ferry pulls away from the dock, loaded up with people, cars, trucks, and pieces of the train that roll aboard on special tracks.

Overhead, the stars brighten. I see a familiar-looking constellation that reminds me of Orion. It's not quite right, though. I squint, my heart speeding up a touch, as if I've just seen someone on the street I'm not sure I recognize.

Is that Orion?

Orion is upside down.

It looks as if he's doing a cartwheel, his sword pointing upward, instead of hanging down at his right knee. I loved astronomy in college, and I know that the Orion nebula is that bright fuzzy bit in his sword. It looks like a star, but it's actually a vast stellar nursery, busily hatching baby suns.

I laugh out loud in delight, then I run inside to get Lala.

She's pleased to see the party version of Orion, but she'd apparently already known this about the heavens. "The moon's upside down too."

I gasp. "*No.*" We can't see it at the moment, but I trust her. How had I not known this? Everyone always asks about the Southern Hemisphere: "Is it true the drain runs the opposite way there?" That's untrue, just a myth.

Nothing has prepared me to see the cosmos upended like this.

This—this land, and this house, and this harbor, and this place—it's all surprising, nothing like I'd pictured when I'd imagined living in Aotearoa.

And it's perfect.

In the same moment, a thought hits me with a thud like I've fallen out of a tree. I struggle to get my wind back as I consider that our search for a new home started in February, when we decided to move around the world. It's now November, and we're finally home.

So...

What the *hell* are we supposed to do next?

Chapter 10

How To Make a Friend

A*t Sea*

I'm taking a sailing class, and I *hate* it.

Okay, that's not totally fair. I like the twenty-four-foot sailboat we crew. I love being out on the water and the way the roll of the sea quiets my mind. I like my classmates just fine, though I'm disappointed to learn that none of them seem to be kindred spirits. Simon and Carolyn are fit, hardy, elderly Kiwis, the kind that routinely blow past us when Lala and I are hiking uphill. Kai and Sam are twenty-five, and while they're pretty cute in the way they bond over the fact that they're both taking a te reo Māori language class, they're not going to end up in my friend Rolodex, the thing I'm actively trying to expand.

I do *not* like the instructor, James. He makes me nervous in an uncomfortable, jittery way. He's not the kind of teacher who leads by calm, clear example; he's more of a shouter who yells at you and keeps yelling until you're eventually doing whatever it is the right way out of sheer panic.

No matter what I do, I can't seem to remember to release the ropes hand over hand. When James yells at me to release the jib, my adrenaline spikes, and I uncoil the wraps off the cleat. Speed is important here; the boat is heeling on its side, and I'm part of the problem. *Fast. Faster.*

So the line flies through my hands as the now-flapping sail tugs the sheet free. Logically, I understand that out at sea, letting the rope rip through your hands in a moment of carelessness will rip all the skin off your palms. Hand over hand is safer. This is what James has taught us.

But I've done it wrong. Again. Disgustedly, he groans, "Jesus, not like *that!* How many times do I have to tell you, *hand over hand?*"

The line's already as slack as it can be, but I mime a hand-over-hand with it to show that I heard him. As soon as we reach the middle of the harbor, we're going to practice man-overboard drills, which is good because at the moment, I feel like jumping overboard myself. Then my classmates would have to save me, though, and he'd shout at them too, so it's better to stay on board. Probably.

I swallow the angry tears rising in my throat.

On Land, Five Weeks Before the Sailing Classes Start

Just a couple of weeks after we moved in, I learned what the hell we would do next: unpack. With perfect timing, our ship came in.

Our boxes were hauled up the fifty steps by the moving company we hired to do the heavy lifting. The team that arrived was made up of one strong, young, *very* hungover man and his elderly uncle, so it didn't go quickly. I felt so guilty about the wheezing old man that I made him sit in the window seat, handing him glass after glass of water. I took his place, carrying boxes up the uneven four flights of stairs. I was grateful none of us died.

A couple of weeks later? *I'm completely unpacked.*

Both suitcases. All the book boxes and all the kitchen boxes. Even my personal boxes are all unpacked, and I have to admit I was really nervous about that part, positive I didn't have enough room in my small office to store everything I'd sent over. I'd felt depressed even thinking about it. *Why* had we shipped so much? I had twenty-six boxes of stuff that were just mine, and I was quite sure I didn't want any of it. So, while the boxes were still in transit, I'd made a decision. I had it all planned out. Sure, I would unbox my clothes and look inside, but then I'd give them all away. I'd just spent six months with exactly enough clothing to get me through a week. It was awesome. Laundry loads were small, and I loved every outfit. I didn't need a single other piece of clothing.

But the strangest thing happened as I opened those boxes.

Every single box was filled with things I liked. No, wait. They were full of things I *loved*. It seemed I'd been ruthless enough when I culled my possessions, because it was as if each box had been packed by an ideal personal shopper. Every item I pulled out delighted me. Oh, here was the Eeyore stuffed animal my sister made me many years ago. Here were all the books I still want to read and haven't yet, carefully curated by a person who intimately knew my reading tastes. Each dress was exactly my size, all of them in great shape, no holes, no baggy bits. Every pair of shoes was comfortable and stylish and so very *me*.

And everything has a place! I have enough storage, and my office doesn't feel cluttered, like it did in the old house. The only three boxes that stayed packed after being opened were the ones holding photos—god knows, someday I want to deal with them, but that time isn't now.

As I type, the windows are open to the summer breeze, and the pōhutukawa tree is shaking its crimson Christmas pompoms high overhead. Here, we open the windows by pushing them outward, then we lock them in place with a metal rod on the inside so the ever-present Wellington wind doesn't smash the glass to bits. Even if screens were a thing in New Zealand, which they don't seem to be, they'd be impossible to add to this kind of Wellington window, so bees and other small flying things bumble in and out on the warm wind. The bees are as big as chihuahuas and while I'd *prefer* they stay out of my office, they're slow and furry and usually mind their own business. I've only been stung once so far, and it was totally my fault as I flapped a bee off my sweater and up my skirt. (I have regrets.) So the bumblers bumble and I'm more careful now about flapping sweaters.

It feels good, all of this.

No, it feels great.

A sensible person would simply say to herself, *Rest, Rachael. Enjoy your new place in time and space.*

This Rachael, though, is not sensible, and she was born with one foot in the future with plans enough to manufacture an extra universe if someone needs a spare.

What next?

Friends.

Now that we're finally well and truly settled in the city we love, we desperately need friends. It's our next important mission. I've made a couple through my twelve-step meeting and a few more through my writers' group, but we have no friends as a couple yet.

Today we've been invited for an afternoon of board games at a stranger's house. The host, Erica, is acquainted with a writer friend of mine in the States, and after an email of introduction, she asks if we'd like to come over. Lala and

I, both shy, gird our loins and go. We take the motorway out of the nation's capital, which sounds like a big deal but feels like a small-town drive. In California, it took twenty minutes of hectic, defensive driving across eight lanes of traffic just to get to the closest grocery store, where parking was a battle of wit and cunning. Here, to get across Wellington proper, from our house to my favorite swimming pool on the other side of town, it takes ten minutes on surface streets. The city is a tiny, walkable jewel, and things are just easier here. The other day while running errands, we had lunch, got a prescription filled, picked up groceries, *and* stopped by the best museum in the country to see the Rita Angus show. Each piece of our afternoon was easy and quick. I've been saying life feels about fifty percent easier here, and Lala says she thinks it's closer to seventy percent.

Know what's not easy, though? Making friends as adults.

We leave the northern end of Wellington and head up the coast to Belmont, an eighteen-minute drive through rolling green hills dotted with sheep and a few cows.

I park in front of the low, white house, which is surrounded by massive flowering bushes on the front. Behind it rises a wilderness of green bush.

"I'm nervous," I say.

Lala nods. "We can still leave."

Instead, we grimace at each other and get out.

No one answers our knock on the door that stands open, so after a minute or two of dithering, we enter, kicking off our shoes and leaving them in the pile of sneakers and sandals in the foyer. As we walk through the house, I inject false confidence into my voice. "Hello! There are strangers coming through your house! We are now in your living room!"

The sound of conversation rises ahead of us, and we follow it into a large kitchen. Seven people sit around a dining room table, and as we enter, they all turn, like a shoal of fish, to look at us.

I'm a *bit* less introverted than Lala, so it's my job to grin and wave. "Hi, I'm Rachael! This is my wife, Lala! We don't know anyone here!"

A woman rises and shakes our hands. "I'm Erica." She's wearing a leather vest over a red corset with a knee-length leather skirt. Her dark hair is scraped back into a ponytail. The way she stands, hips square and hands hanging ready, makes me wonder if she's one of the horse girls who grew up. I swing my gaze around the room and spot with considerable satisfaction not one, but *two* horse paintings. I will bet every New Zealand dollar I have that she painted them herself.

She introduces us to the others, and then, it gets awkward.

Really, really awkward.

Erica moves out of the room to talk to her husband, who appears to be hiding in a small bedroom just off the kitchen. Because she's left the room, there's one open chair at the table, but we don't want to take hers. I shuffle around a bit, looking for more chairs and end up hauling in a rolling office chair with a broken arm from another room, and Lala brings in an old-fashioned carved wooden chair.

We sit. I reach for a bit of bread and dip it in the hummus on the table, but the chatting is so sparse I'm sure they can hear my molars grinding on the crust.

"So," I manage. "What do you all like to play?"

A husband and wife (also American) look at each other with an expression I don't understand, then the man says,

"Oh, we like to play all the things. Got a whip or a cat-o'-nine tails? We'll play."

I choke on the bread, and the wife laughs.

Finally, I manage, "Funny. Yep. Ha. That's funny." It's not funny, actually, but I've got nothing else. "So for real, what games? We like Carcassonne, and Zombie Dice, and Lala likes Pandemic, but that's a little too real now, am I right? Lala's the game player, honestly. She goes to game conventions and everything. She plays everything. I'm just the knitter." I waggle my knitting bag at them and pull out my sock-in-progress. "See? I knit. I'll play if I have to, but honestly, I prefer to watch."

I only have myself to blame when the American guy winks and says, "That can be arranged."

The single Kiwi woman across from me seems to take pity on me, saying, "We never get around to playing games here. We just sit around and talk. Mostly about sex." She has bright green hair and her voice is loud.

The other two men at the end of the table are introduced as Erica's Kiwi coworkers. Their cheeks are now bright red, and both stare into their beer bottles as if they've seen a way out at the bottom. If they have, I'm almost willing to throw away four years without a drink to join them in the search.

After approximately ninety-three hours, Erica comes back and takes her position at the head of the table. She, the Kiwi woman, and the American couple spend the next *two hours* talking about the places in the world they like better than New Zealand, and various fetishes.

And honestly, my dismay is not about the kink talk. I like kinksters. I just don't like *these* ones. How do they not love living in New Zealand? How is that even possible? I have to admit, the moment I begin to enjoy myself is when I give up on making friends with any of them. I will not exchange phone numbers or emails. My last name will remain a secret, and no Instagram handles will be traded. Nope, I'm just going to watch, so it's probably good I've already established myself as that kind of person.

I lean back in the broken office chair, tuck my legs under myself, and knit my way through three ginger ales, making mental notes about these characters, pledging to steal and use them in my writing someday. Later, Lala tells me that the Kiwi woman was hitting on me, but I don't notice it in the moment. The woman does say something about falling through a ceiling into a bed with me, but I change the subject to cover the fact that I have no idea what the hell she's talking about. The Kiwi coworkers' eyes get bigger and bigger, especially when the American pulls out his cell phone to show off pictures of the dungeon he left behind in Nevada.

No game ever hits the table. I'm not certain there are any games in the house at all.

Finally, we've been here a polite-enough length of time that I'll be able to tell my writer friend in the States that we did, in fact, meet Erica, and wow, yes, we did! Indeed!

Lala's soul has left her body as she stares at a nail hole in the wall opposite her, and I have to tug on her arm to get her to realize that I'm packing up my knitting.

My voice is a chirp. "Well, then, thanks, *this* was fun!"

There are hugs and promises to stay in touch, to do it again sometime soon.

When we get in the car, I pant, clutching the wheel. "What was that? What just happened?"

Lala is pale. "I have never enjoyed not playing games less."

"Agree. Hard agree. But we need friends," I say. Now

that we live in Wellington, making friends is what matters most. "We *need* them."

She rubs her eyes and I wonder if she's about to cry, but then she laughs so hard I have to join her. Together, we howl with laughter for a couple of minutes. "But really," she eventually says, dabbing at her streaming eyes, trying to catch her breath. "*Do* we?"

At Sea

"Man overboard!" James yells, tossing a horseshoe-shaped life preserver over the sailboat's stern. The life preserver is our stand-in for an actual body in the water—this is a drill, and we're practicing sailing the boat in a rough figure eight to pick up the "person" who's fallen out.

I want to object to the sexist term—I am not a man, and if we held a vote, I know I'd be voted Most Likely to Fall Overboard. But I say nothing. The drill has started, and my pulse is already racing even though I'm only the starboard trimmer and likely won't have to do anything but tighten a rope, if that. (Pardon me, I mean "trim the jib sheet if we're sailing on a port tack"—the terminology is still overwhelming.) In my mind, I chant *hand over hand*.

Sam is on helm and pushes us into a broad reach. Rain hits our faces, but none of us move to adjust our jackets. We're busy doing the sailing work as James shouts important things. We let out the sails so that they get more purchase on the wind and Carolyn, the spotter, keeps her eyes on the life preserver with her arm extended, pointing right at it, so that Sam can see exactly where our lost crew member is.

James barks, "Bear away!"

Sam's blank expression matches all of ours. "Huh?"

Our instructor rolls his eyes. "Bear *away* from the wind!"

I can tell that Sam is just guessing as he pushes the tiller away from himself.

Sure enough, James bellows, "*Pull* the tiller! Bear *away* from the wind!"

Sam does it right, then we get into position to do a tack. I trim the jib and cling to the lifeline as the boat heels over onto its side. In the wind, the boat's sway is violent, though the gusts aren't even that high today in this, the windiest city in the world.

Sam's got it under control now, and we're sailing directly toward the poor, wet life preserver.

James yells, "Boat hook!"

Everyone looks at me, the trimmer currently with nothing to trim. This is my moment! I spring into action, hurl myself down the short ladder into the hold, and find the boat hook. Just as I lift it, a gust catches the mainsail and my feet lurch out from under me.

I fly into the air, and as I fall, the boat heaves the other way. I land on my back, hitting my head on a bench.

Taking a split second to breathe, I shake my head. My shoulder is screaming, but it was hurting before class, a strained muscle from swimming. I struggle to stand. I've got to go back up there, but oh, how I wish I could just stay down here. I want to throw myself under the genoa sail tucked in the hold and hide until we're firmly docked.

On Land, Two Weeks Before the Sailing Classes Start

Everyone is out and about, enjoying the bright summer morning in the central business district of Wellington. Restaurants are full, people spilling onto the sidewalks and sitting at tables covered with coffee cups and plates of waffles. A cloud of cinnamon-scented air blows out of a bakery, and three small children stand in the middle of the sidewalk, ecstatically pulling apart a large sweet roll.

But I'm coated with dread, my hands dripping with it. "We don't have to stay long. Thirty minutes if it's bad."

Lala says, "No matter what, it can't be as bad as the non-game party."

"But what if it is? We could just leave now, send a text, and go to the beach."

"We're almost there. Let's just meet them." This is brave of Lala to say, since she wants to be here even less than I do.

The invite came out of the blue from a woman named Olivia. She'd seen a post of mine on Instagram, and in a DM, she said she and her wife lived in Wellington and would be happy to get a coffee and give us some local recommendations. "Obviously I understand having some random person from the internet contacting you is probably a bit weird, so totally understand if you're not keen :)"

I *was* keen! I immediately messaged her back, but at this very moment, I'm regretting every social impulse I've ever had. I obviously can't be trusted. Olivia and her partner will probably try to sell us LuLaRoe or talk us into joining a cult. It's such a small town; they probably know Erica.

We trudge toward our doom, a short block away.

As we arrive, we get two cheerful waves from two nice, normal-looking women, but I trust nothing now. Most likely they're hiding a stack of religious tracts behind their backs, getting ready to thrust them upon us along with the word of our lord and savior.

Olivia and Leticia reach forward to introduce themselves. Their hands appear empty, tract-less.

Just then, a bee flies in front of Lala's face.

An important thing to know about Lala is that she's phobic of bees. She's not allergic, as far as she knows (but she's never been stung, as she always points out, so she very well *could* be). If one flies near, her body will immediately relocate itself to a place four or five hundred feet away. This requires no planning on her part—the bodily extrication just occurs, spontaneously. I've seen her knock over chairs (and once, a table), in her flight of the bumblebee.

She's never run directly into traffic in one of her impromptu exoduses but since we're standing on a narrow sidewalk on a busy street, I feel this is the moment she might lose that bragging right. I see the bee before she does, so I plant myself between her and the edge of the street, in case her impending getaway throws her trafficward.

She sees the bee. Immediately, she performs a mighty, six-part sneeze-breakdance move that takes her to me, away from me, toward the diners on the sidewalk, and finally, a block and a half down the street.

And it turns out, her dance is exactly the icebreaker we need. Olivia and Leticia respond beautifully, with thoughtful concern. They don't laugh. (I can't claim this strength of character.) We abandon the crowded place where we'd planned to eat and cross the street to a restaurant with available indoor and blessedly insect-free tables.

After ordering coffee and cheese scones, we chat. Soft-spoken, kind-eyed Olivia has the same kind of web development job as Lala, and they share an immediate language. Smiling Aussie Leticia is wearing a cute jumpsuit she sewed herself that fits her perfectly, so we share a language too. We talk, all around the table, about everything: crafts, travel, Wellington, swimming. They have a sailboat, which thrills me.

Leticia leans forward, her eyes sparkling. "Oh, do you sail?"

I snort. "Well, I grew up sailing on my dad's boats, but since I usually had to bail, I think I'm a little traumatized. And I once took sailing lessons in Oakland, but it was a really short course, and I've forgotten most of what I learned. I'm dying to learn here, but I'm scared of the Wellington wind."

"Oh, you *have* to take a class! We loved the one we took."

"And then you can crew for us." Olivia says this like it's no big deal. "We have a couple of friends taking the class starting on Tuesday. Maybe there's another spot?"

My heart leaps, and I taste joy that has nothing to do with the cheese scone. I like these people so much, and not because they're some of the only people I know here. I would like them no matter where I met them, but they're here, and oh, please, can we keep them? Please?

Later, Lala and I walk a block without speaking, in case they're watching us leave. We don't want to lose our cool too soon.

Then, when we're far enough away, I clutch Lala's arm and hiss, "I love them."

"Me too."

We share a delighted look.

I ask, "Do we actually have friends?"

Her eyes widen. "I think we have *friends*."

At home, I build up just enough courage to try to join the sailing class their friends are in, but it's full. In our kitchen, I sigh and look down at the harbor full of whitecaps and tossing boats. I watch the weekly Rum Race head out, a small fleet of sailboats exiting the marina, all of them sharply heeled over in the high winds. I imagine terrified crew clinging to stanchions and crying (isn't that what sailors do?) and I'm grateful I'm not down there with them.

My phone buzzes with a text. *Kia ora, Rachael, sorry that class was full, but we've just opened another, starting next Tuesday. Here's the link to join.*

No.

Nope.

Just look at that wind. It's terrifying, what those sailors are doing out there. I've been doing scary things now for almost a year, and I'm tired of frightening myself. I don't need to fight the goddamn ocean too.

But...I love being on the water so much.

I hear Olivia's voice in my head. *Then you can crew for us.*

Sailing on a boat that belongs to friends. My throat tight, I navigate from the text message to the Buy button, clicking before I can talk myself out of it again.

At Sea

Below deck, I'm getting my bearings after my fall. I'm a bit dizzy, but the boat hook is still in my hand, and the drowning life preserver has to be saved. I rush up the companionway onto the deck. Carolyn's arm is still pointing directly at the "man," and Sam's doing a good job of steering.

Kai, the other trimmer, says, "Saw you. Nice one." His eyes are laughing, and good for him. Every pratfall should make someone laugh. And because I'm pretty damn sure if I lean overboard to reach for the life preserver, I *will* end up needing it myself, I give the boat hook to Kai.

James sneers. "Passing off your duty to someone else, huh?"

"I sure am." I don't remind him about my injured shoulder, something I already mentioned at the beginning of tonight's sail.

The boat comes alongside the life preserver, and Kai reaches out and down. In doing so, he somehow manages to tug the red handle of his own life vest.

Pop, pop, pop, POP.

Kai's torso is immediately surrounded by multiple yellow floats as his vest inflates explosively, but he still manages to haul up the life preserver. The man overboard is finally safe, and Kai triumphantly holds the life preserver aloft, his arms high above his expanded vest.

We all laugh, then James orders us to make a rotation. I want to be the spotter—never have I felt more ready to do something on board a boat. I will keep my eyes on the prize! My arm will point, straight and sure! My other hand will grip something tightly, and no matter how hard the boat rolls, I will stay onboard! But instead, he chooses me to helm for the next round.

I slide onto the bench to hold the tiller, and in a minor miracle, I actually understand what James is saying most of the time. My hands are still shaking from the fall, but I don't think anyone notices. As the light but steady rain seeps down my neck, the boat goes where I want it to, and the unlucky life preserver is saved. Then we swap places and repeat it again, and again.

Back in the classroom, I nod along as James goes over what we just did. I push down my wish that he would teach us first, before showing us, but that's not his way. The fact that my learning style doesn't jibe with his is okay since everyone else in the class seems to be a hands-on learner unshaken by shouting.

Me, though? My gut is tight, and I break the clip on my

pen as I take notes. As soon as James starts putting away the magnetic boats that tack and gybe up and down the classroom whiteboard, I give a tight wave to everyone and force my voice to be bright. "See you Tuesday!"

In the car, as the rain pounds down in earnest, I fail at swallowing back the tears. Furious with myself, I start the car and head for home, but I'm not sure if the traffic lights waver because of the water on my windshield or in my eyes. I park and climb the staircase to our flat. Lala is in the tub. While I take off my shoes, she calls out, "How did it go, my little sailor?"

I kneel at the tub and cry as she pats my head.

"What happened? Are you okay?"

My throat is too tight to speak.

"Rachael. You're scaring me. Talk."

"I fell." It's stupid, and it's not what I'm upset about, but they are the only words I can find.

She strokes my face, wiping away a tear. "Oh, no! Did you hurt yourself?"

Every time I go out on the class's sailboat, I come home with enormous bruises on my knees and arms and stranger places, like my belly and inner thigh. But falling didn't hurt me any more than normal. "I don't think so. I'll have some extra bruises, and my shoulder still hurts, but I'm okay."

"And you didn't fall overboard..."

I put my head on my knees. "No."

"So..." Her voice is gentle. "Why are you so upset, then?"

"I don't want to go back."

"But you love sailing."

She is wrong. At the moment, I do not love sailing. I hate the class with the way its boat goes out in the harbor so full of *wind*, and I hate the teacher and how he's right for everyone but me, and at the moment, I hate all of my four classmates except for Kai because he laughed appropriately when I fell, and I got to laugh at him and his stupid exploding life vest. "I want to quit."

"You can."

I raise my head. She's not supposed to say that. "What?"

"You don't have to go back. You're an adult. You don't have to do anything you don't want to."

"But I'm being stupid. I'm just scared." *That's* why I'm crying, I realize. I was scared out there, in the wind and my slippery-soled sneakers. I was terrified that I'd fall, picturing myself plunging overboard into the cold water, and then I confirmed the worry by losing my balance so suddenly below deck, and I only understood about half of what James shouted, even though I'd been studying at home and watching sailing videos on YouTube, and I hated being in the tiny, overheated classroom after the sail, and all of it just came down to one simple fact: I was scared.

Lala says, "What about—"

But I'm already up and moving out of the bathroom. "Sorry. I'll let you have your bath."

I go to my desk and take a breath. Then I send an SOS.

Hi Olivia and Leticia, I NEED YOU TO TALK ME OFF THE LEDGE. Are you free tomorrow for coffee?

On Land, Two Weeks After the Sailing Classes Start

We meet at the Chocolate Fish, a cafe on the other side of the harbor from our kitchen window. I peek at the building sometimes through the binoculars. I like its outdoor section, with all the tables and chairs and things for kids to play with, scooters and tricycles that they throw into reckless skids as their parents talk with friends.

We are here with *our* friends, Olivia and Leticia.

I don't cry. It surprises me that I don't even want to, that I laugh about James and the shouting and the falling, even though the night before everything felt so dire. "It feels so treacherous, the surface of the boat. I know there's such a thing as boat shoes. Do I need those? I've just been wearing trainers." It's fun to say that word, to abandon the word *sneaker*. Lala and I have agreed, privately, that saying things like motorway and togs instead of freeway and swimsuit isn't pretentious but honorable. We live here now, and we want people to understand us, so we'll use their words.

Leticia shakes her head. "What size shoe are you?"

"Thirty-nine-ish?"

"I'll lend you my old boat shoes. They're beat up, but they'll stick to the deck way better than trainers."

"I'd *love* to borrow them."

Olivia says, "And you should borrow my sailing gloves. They'll help a lot when you're pulling lines."

Hand over hand.

We talk about everything for a long time, and by the time we leave, the air has cooled enough for me to need the sweater I didn't wear at the table. I'm astonished to realize that three hours have slipped by. I have a preternaturally good sense of time, no matter what, and I rarely lose even a minute, let alone hours. I would have sworn we'd been chatting for no more than ninety minutes.

"Three *hours*," I say in the car.

"We have friends," Lala responds.

"And we like them so *much*."

At Sea

On Tuesday, I'm back in class. I have decided I will give

this one more shot, then I can quit with no guilt if I still want to.

In the middle of the harbor, the winds pick up and a light drizzle starts. But in Leticia's shoes, my feet stick to the deck like I've become a gecko. James puts me on bow duty, and I have to hoist the mainsail and the jib. I don't fall overboard, and Olivia's sailing gloves protect my palms even though I don't forget to hand-over-hand.

We sail.

As we do, James tells tall sailing stories, and he doesn't yell, not even once. Maybe that's because his crew finally understands enough to not be a hazard to themselves—maybe he can finally relax and enjoy the movement of the boat in the wind.

He points. "Here they come."

A pod of dolphins, just off the starboard bow. My heart clenches in my chest as they leap, dazzling, in a ray of late sun that breaks through the clouds. They play in our wake, diving under the boat and coming up on the other side, splashing and soaring.

Kai asks James, "Do you ever get tired of seeing them?"

"Never. The day you get tired of seeing dolphins, of being on the water, is the day you retire, mate." Then he goes on to tell us about how the day you buy a boat is the second-happiest day of your life, right after the first happiest day of your life, the day you sell it. He's already told this joke three times, but this is the first time I think it's hilarious, and as a dolphin leaps just yards from my hand, I laugh out loud.

I reach toward the dolphin, as if I'm holding a herring, as if the dolphin is trained and will come kiss my fingers to get its snack.

James is watching me, looking worried.

I pull back. "Don't worry," I say. "I'm not going overboard today."

Kai says, "But then we'd get to practice the man-overboard drill again, and I wouldn't mind a bit more practice. So yeah, Rachael, go ahead."

With a shake of his head, James says, "Screw all that. One of you numpties goes overboard, we drop the sails, turn on the motor, go back and fish you out. Easy as that."

Oh, my god. Of course we would. Why hadn't that occurred to me?

He goes on, "Sure, it's good to know how to sail back for someone, but when something bad happens, we do the easiest, fastest thing to get a friend out of trouble."

I stand on the deck and wiggle my feet in the shoes, which are a tiny bit tight but reassuringly so. My palms are warm and protected by the borrowed gloves. My legs are strong, and so are my eyes—when I gaze westward, I can't *quite* make out my house, but I can see the glen where it sits, facing the water. Sometimes Lala takes pictures of the boat I'm on by pointing the lens of her iPhone's camera through the binoculars in the kitchen. She might be doing that right now, so I give a surreptitious wave homeward.

I turn. Over there is where I go to my twelve-step meeting—I can see the shape of the Long Hall from the deck of the boat. On Sunday mornings, I meet my friends there. I turn again, facing north, in the direction of my new and already dear writing friends, Moira and Anne and Ali, who live an hour up the coast. I look back toward our house and know that just over the hill in Johnsonville is where Leticia and Olivia live, who are not just *my* friends but *our* friends.

Unstuck.

We came unstuck.

And then we came here.

We have no roots anymore. But we can still anchor ourselves safely in the port of our choosing.

James shouts, "Rachael, you want to helm us in?"

I do not. Not really. I never want to leave this dolphin-full perfect spot.

But I nod. "Absolutely."

Chapter 11

Naked and Afraid

On Tuesdays, our dog friend Paddy comes to our house to play.

In our rental house, we can't have pets. Heartbreakingly, this is how most rentals in New Zealand are. But our lease says nothing about dogs who visit their friends while their people are at work, does it? No. I've triple-checked, and it does not.

We meet Paddy the way most matches start these days: on an online dating site. The Dog Share Collective is like a library for New Zealand dog lovers who want to borrow local dogs as if they're fluffy books. When we see Paddy's face on the site, it's love at first sight. A wildly smart springer spaniel, he's the best-trained dog we've ever met. We live in fear of sending him home a chain-smoking gambling addict, but that doesn't stop us from spoiling him to within an inch of his spaniel life. For the first time in our adult lives, we have no pets, and therefore, no vet bills. This is Paddy's gain: he has an entire shelf in the living room just for his toys, and I love to watch him shred his most-beloved duck while splayed on his back on the floor of my office. As soon as he deconstructs a toy to free-floating atoms and puffs of fiberfill, we head down to Animates and let him fill up the cart with bourbon and bison burgers.

Paddy's owner April says that his favorite place in the world is the top of a green space in the Wellington Town Belt near our house. There, he can be off-leash to chase a ball or a stick, which is what he was born to do. Well, that's fine for him. He's got four strong legs and a play drive equivalent to that of a toddler with a new Big Wheel and an uncapped two-liter bottle of Coke.

But for the two-legged animal who's walking Paddy, the hike up to the top of the hill is a long, steep climb through the bush, which includes an almost-eight-hundred-foot elevation gain. I haven't yet made it to the very tippety-top, where Paddy can run free.

Today, I'm determined I'll make it all the way up with my eager pal.

As I clip on Paddy's leash, I look out the dining room windows at the dark clouds rolling in from the south over the harbor, and think, *huh! It looks like rain!* Then I check all four of my favorite weather apps, all of which exclaim, *Nope! No rain coming this way, no way, no how.* And like the rank amateur I am to living in New Zealand, I believe them.

The first half of the walk goes well. Paddy has to stay on lead for the on-trail part, and he's a strong puller, so I hurtle forward faster than I would without him.

The trail I've picked to attempt the summit of Te Ahumairangi is magnificent, winding through ancient trees and towering ferns. The mamaku ferns, in particular, look straight out of *Jurassic Park*. They can grow up to five stories high and have hexagonal black trunks and furry fiddleheads the size of a large man's hand. As I hike, I peek through the trees and catch glimpses of downtown Wellington, the tall buildings with their glimmering windows far below. I love this, because I'm only a casual hiker, preferring to be within easy range of an oat-milk cappuccino, bonus points if I can hike home with a new book.

In fact, I've said many times I'm not a hiker at all. But here, in New Zealand, it's different. Here, so *much* has changed that I feel as if I'm charting the landscape by walking. Maybe by tramping, I'm attempting to navigate the uncertainties of this past year. Perhaps if I walk far enough, if I push myself hard enough up as many hills as it takes, I'll have a better idea of what's behind me and a clearer vision for the future.

Maybe.

So I've bought hiking boots. Real ones, the kind you wear on Hiking Adventures. I've purchased hiking poles, though I haven't used them yet. In fact (and this is scary to admit), Lala and I have signed up to hike the Abel Tasman Track in December, a seventy-kilometer trail that takes five days to trek. We are, of course, doing it the comfortable middle-aged way, and by that, I mean some nice person will transport our bags and hand us a packed lunch at the start of each day. That same someone will pick us up each night and deposit us either in a hotel with a real shower or a fancy glamping tent with sleeping bags we haven't carried on our backs. We're not twenty years old, and sleeping in huts on the trail with snoring strangers while carrying and cooking all our own food—oh, my god, just typing that partial sentence gave me a strong urge to order sushi. One of the things I love best about delivery is that the driver carries the food up the fifty steps to our front door.

Yes, I'm excited about the hike, but I also know that signing up means we have to train. So going out after work for a steep ramble with Paddy is a good idea, I think. Even if it looks like rain. We can do it.

And now we're almost at the top! Paddy is pulling harder because he knows where we're going. It's *obviously* the best place in the world, and he can't wait to show it to me.

A slight drizzle starts, but we're under the thick cover of trees, so it's okay that I've dressed rather inappropriately for a damp hike. Only a few drops scatter through the boughs, and I've lived here long enough to know that Wellington weather changes its mind as fast and often as I change radio stations in the car.

The going is difficult, though, and I'm sweaty and panting as we reach the highest point of the final rise. Paddy, though—the boy is just getting started. His sweet spaniel face is frantic with delight. *Can you believe this luck? Here we are together in what I know is heaven!* Finally, I can let him run, and I do, throwing his favorite stick over and over. Fortuitously, each stick I pick up is his favorite one, the very best stick he's ever seen in his life, well done me.

Then, as we hit the grassy top of the hill, as we emerge from the cover of the trees, the clouds open.

And it rains.

I mean, it *RAINS*. It's Holly-Golightly-in-the-alley kind of rain, it's turkeys-drowning-if-they-look-up kind of rain.

And for some ungodly reason, I've left the house in only a white linen tunic and my stupidest, lightest-weight knee-length leggings. My shoes? They're excellent. Completely waterproof, I've been assured, and so far, my feet do seem to be dry.

But the rest of me? I have no hat or scarf or even a sweatshirt's hood. My only top layer is that linen (again, *white* linen) and the tunic immediately plasters to my body, turning the pale putty color of my skin underneath. Oh, except for my black sports bra, of course, which is as clearly on display through my shirt as my belly rolls are, where the ridiculous (and also surprisingly see-through) leggings pull in a bit too tightly. Please let me be clear: I love my rolls. I love my body. It's strong and healthy and happy. *However.* I'm enough of a prude that I do not relish being functionally naked on a busy trail on which everyone else is dressed like they've heard of weather before. Long raincoats and rain hats. Thick-looking sporty leggings, probably lined. Gloves and scarves, even though we're near the end of summer. One man wears a lime-green balaclava—his cheeks are probably toasty and dry. My own cheeks are covered with clumps of mascara and rivers of rain, and I only know this because the clumps keep washing into my mouth, sour and gritty.

I am naked and stupid and miserable. I'm also getting colder by the second as the rain buckets down harder and the southerly picks up, howling over the top of the hill, straight off the Antarctic (seriously).

Paddy—lord love him—runs and runs. He doesn't care that I'm freezing and miserable and as liable to die of embarrassment as exposure. Or maybe of embarrassment *at* the exposure.

The problem is getting worse: my new boots are definitely waterproof because, even though they're tightly tied, the endless downpour is violent enough to fill them from the top. No water is leaking out, no sir, so now the puddles I'm trudging through are strapped directly to my feet.

And because I was so goddamn set on making it to the

top of the hill for the first time, I walked so far that it's still a forty-five-minute walk to Paddy's house, where I'm supposed to drop him off, followed by a thirty-minute walk home. Alternately, I could walk home to our car and drive Paddy to his house, but the car is also a forty-five-minute walk away in a different direction.

And those forty-five minutes? They're mostly along city streets that are filling up with people coming home from work (Wellington is a city that walks, even in the rain). I'm getting colder and colder by the second. At least I can't get any wetter, I suppose. But I simply can't bear the thought of shivering through the rain and being seen by a hundred people, all of whom judge me (correctly) to be a huge naked idiot who doesn't understand the basic function of clothing.

I can't jump on the bus because of Paddy.

No Uber will pick up a person and a dog this wet.

So I call Lala.

Logistically, this isn't easy to do with my waterlogged phone. It keeps wanting to connect to my drenched AirPods that are refusing to turn off properly. So Lala can hear me but I can't hear her, then that switches: she's loud and clear to me but she can't hear a word I'm saying.

Emotionally, it's not easy to ask either. I *hate* to be rescued. I am the rescuer. Never the rescued. This is clearly printed on the box I came in, right next to This Way Up. But we can finally hear each other well enough that I can ask for help.

The asking isn't even the biggest problem.

Lala hasn't driven in Wellington yet. The streets here are notoriously difficult to navigate. People park on both sides of the cramped streets, leaving only the narrowest lane for single cars to squeak through. On trash days, it's not uncommon to hear the rubbish truck honking until someone runs out of their house and moves their car so the truck can scrape by. The streets are *supposed* to support two-way traffic, but in reality, it's a constant game of telepathically deciding with a stranger who should back up to allow the other one to pass. Usually on a tight curve. Learning to do all of this while sitting on the right and driving on the left is intense (backing up while looking over the wrong shoulder, especially, is hard to learn).

Honestly, I like doing all the driving, and yes, at some point, Lala wants to be comfortable on the roads here. But we haven't really had a *need* for her to drive. Until this moment.

To make it worse, night is falling, and this is the biggest rainstorm we've seen in this rainy, windy city. Also, I'm asking her to pick me up on a street we never drive on, so she'll have to figure out how to zigzag her way here on tiny, busy streets she hasn't even experienced as a passenger.

In an act of true love, she agrees to rescue me and Paddy just as my phone sputters out.

By now I'm shivering and trying not to cry. I'm an idiot, I hate myself, and I'm even angry with poor, sweet Paddy who *just wants to fetch the stick.* But I put him back on the leash, and we tumble, heartbreakingly stickless, down the mountain toward the road where Lala will pick us up. I leave the trails and we break through the bush, being whapped by tree limbs, dodging low vines and muddy holes, and now I *am* crying, although no one would be able to tell, and it's all horrible.

And *this* is why I hate hiking.

I abhor it. I'll never do it again. Ever.

Staggering off the trail and out onto the road, I head for the corner where I told Lala we'd be.

Someone honks behind us.

Paddy's owner April pulls over in her boxy little wagon.

She's headed home from work, and impossibly, she's taken this side road, only to find me and her very own dog skidding gracelessly homeward.

I gasp and gibber. "Yes, please, a ride home, *yes*. But can you please—oh, can you text Lala? My phone is too wet to work, and she's coming to get me, but she's never driven in Wellington and only a few times in New Zealand at all, and it's getting dark, and what if she can't find me—maybe you shouldn't drive me home. Just take Paddy. Yeah? Should I wait for her here? But what if I told her the wrong place, wait, did I even tell her the right street name? What am I going to do? Oh, no, how will I *find* her?"

I'm a catastrophizer under stress—it's one of my least favorite traits. The knock at the door must be the downstairs neighbor saying there's a gas leak and we must evacuate before the explosion. A loved one running five minutes late is the sure sign they've sailed over a cliff. So as I soak April's car seat with the frigid water streaming off my goosebumps, I'm completely convinced that Lala will be unable to find me and then she'll die in the wreck that inevitably occurs because she's not used to the car/rain/streets/Japanese-language-stereo. I'll never see her alive again, and it will be all my fault.

April says simply, "I'll text her."

Wait, Lala must have already left the house, and April's *text* will be what distracts her, and oh, my god—

But Lala hasn't left the house, nor has she even seen April's text yet when we pull up. She's just coming down our steps (sensibly clad in her bright red raincoat).

I jabber a grateful goodbye to April and to the bedraggled but happily exhausted Paddy, and upstairs, I take off my boots and pour the water out of them as Lala watches.

I look at my wife, overcome by how much I love her. At how much she loves *me*. She was willing to drive out to rescue me in a storm on streets she doesn't know in a country in which she doesn't drive.

My absolute hero. What a lucky woman I am.

"Why didn't you wear a jacket?" she asks.

The shift from rhapsody to irritation feels as good as slamming my kneecap into a dining chair in the dark. "Because I *checked* the weather. All four of my apps agreed there would be no rain, and they never agree."

"Didn't it look like rain, though? It's been looking like rain for hours."

I spit through gritted teeth, "*That's why I checked the weather apps.*" Hang on. She's still my hero. "You get to take all the credit and you didn't even need to do the work. My knight in shining red raincoat."

I wait for her to say, *You're so welcome. Anything for my beloved.*

Instead, she says, "Yeah, well, next time take a jacket, how about?"

I stomp into the bathroom, where I peel off my clothes. They slap heavily onto the floor along with my mood.

I run the tub full and hot.

As I lie in the water, I hear Lala moving around the kitchen. It's her turn to cook, and she's making us chicken and roast potatoes for dinner. She laughs at the podcast playing in her (dry) AirPods, and I smell garlic and thyme.

I realize I am safe.

I had been so cold and so embarrassed and so alone and now I'm none of those things.

Nothing bad happened. Probably nothing bad would have happened even if I'd walked all the way home. The embarrassment wouldn't have actually killed me.

I am loved. I am home.

A few days later, I make the hike again, this time without Paddy. Not only do I check the weather (dry, all the apps swear-to-god-hope-to-die) but I also take a jacket. Take that, Weather!

Walking up the trails without Paddy yanking me toward sticklandia is decidedly less exciting but much easier. This time, I can look around and enjoy the way the trees bend, the way the late afternoon light filters yellow and heavy through the leaves. Two large kākā squabble in the sky above me, and a tūī flaps past, singing its robotic song.

In the smack-dab middle of the bush, I have to make a decision. More steep climbing to the very top, to the dizzying views of the harbor? Or down, to the city street far below that holds both a cafe and my favorite bookshop? I'm a hiker now—I walk out my front door, and the map I'm making stretches out in front of me, both physically and mentally. I get to make the decision that's best for me in this very moment.

I decide: I will head up to the top.

My nice dry boots dig into the mulched leaves for a while. Pausing, I squat to examine a hairy spider and then a curious white mushroom that looks like a honeycomb-shaped dog toy. (I find out later it's a basket fungus called tūtae kēhua, or "poo from a ghost.")

I hike to where the trees open to grass and pure, blue sky. Then I look down and my gaze traces the streets below, reading their signs in my mind: Sar Street, Lennel Road, Sefton and Anne, Fitzroy and Hutt. Down there, if you turn right on Park, you'll pass our favorite grocery store, which is just down the street from where our prime minister works. I spend a pleasant moment imagining Jacinda nipping over at lunchtime for a bottle of milk and a Cadbury bar, before plotting my way back home in my mind, deciding which trails and streets I'll take.

Up here, I'm both hiker and cartographer. I'm the rescuer who is rescued. I'm the finder of the best sticks, the wearer of the raincoat, and the girl who has always splashed and will always splash in puddles, even if she has to carry them with her inside her boots. I'm the overreactor, the worrier, the buyer of excellent dog toys, the swimmer, the writer, and the one who is so full of gratitude her veins ache with it at least three times a day.

The map I'm making says I'm home. Which is good, because I'm hungry and tonight, it's my turn to cook.

I turn and head toward Lala.

Chapter 12

A Day In Wellington

One year ago, as we got off the bus that whisked us from the Auckland airport to our quarantine hotel, I tugged the edge of my mask away from my face. I knew I wasn't supposed to, but I had to. Just for a second. I inhaled. I might have gasped a bit. Ah, there it was —that first scent of clean, rain-washed Auckland air lightly mixed with the exhaust from the motorway. We'd made it. Our feet were finally on Aotearoa soil. I would have kneeled and kissed it, but that would have drawn the guards' attention to me, and I was already pushing my luck stealing my sneaky inhalation.

How do we celebrate today, our first anniversary of starting our new life?

First, I make a cup of tea. Green, with lemon and ginger. I pour it into my Welly Girl mug, a favorite of mine. On it, a woman in red rain boots is being blown by the famous Wellington wind, her white hair whipping sideways.

Then I go into the living room and sit by the window that overlooks the harbor. Because it's the middle of winter and because I get up early, it's still dark. I light two candles, which give me just enough light to see the nib of my fountain pen moving against the page. I light one candle for me, and one for creativity, asking it to come close and sit by me.

I write my morning pages as the sun slowly rises over the water. The kākā screech, flapping past the window in the brightening sky. My own heart flaps in a similar ridiculous way.

Thirty minutes pass, my pen scratching at the paper of my spiral-bound notebook. The cover says, "The Moon Made Me Do It," and I'm filling it with my favorite violet ink. They're rubbish thoughts, just stream-of-consciousness stuff, but it feels good to flip the pages I've already permanently marked. In purple ink, I was here.

My phone pings with a text. It's April. *Leaving now*.

I send back a puppy and a heart-eyes emoji before rushing to the kitchen to bag up the trash. Normally when April brings Paddy over on Tuesday mornings, it reminds me to take down the yellow bag at the same time as I meet them downstairs. But since last week April's husband had Covid, there was no Paddy and I forgot about trash day. Today I manage to get two weeks of rubbish to fit into just one $3.10 garbage bag, so I'm feeling pleased with myself as I head down the stairs into the winter rain. Could we afford to use another bag? Yes. Am I cheap? Also yes.

After placing the bag on the side of the road, I tug my rain hat tightly onto my head and cross the road to wait for April's car. This is the first time I've ever lived in a place with real weather, and I'm convinced rain hats are the best thing ever. I hate the way raincoat hoods slide around and off, or, if they're tight enough to fit well, they expose your face, and my mascara leaps off my lashes at the mere suggestion of a raindrop's existence. But my black bucket hat that's cute, waterproof, and practical? I wear it every chance I get.

I lean over the railing and look out at the water. It's choppy today after the storm that roared through overnight, but a pale blue gleam to the south makes me think that if he's lucky, Paddy might get a good dry walk later. I turn around and look up the hill and at our windows, high above. The rain is slackening off, and it's lighter now, but it's still dark enough that the candles burn brightly in the window.

I lit those. That's *our* window.

Okay, it's a rental house, and therefore, it's not really ours. I know someday we won't live here anymore. This unbelievable view won't always be right in front of us, which makes the view even more precious. Would I take all this glory for granted if it was actually "mine?" Would the beauty wear off? Maybe it's better this way.

April pulls up, and I open the back door of her green car. Paddy, that good boy, whaps his tail enthusiastically against the seat but doesn't jump out. He waits for me to give him the green light.

"Okay."

When he's at my side, I speak over the back seat. "How's Jules feeling?"

April grins. "So much better. He's back to work again."

"And you never got it?"

"Nope." She'd quarantined elsewhere after Jules tested positive. "Can you believe it?"

I can. She works at the hospital, and they've taken Covid precautions seriously from the very start. She hands me Paddy's lunch, and with a wave, she's gone.

Once upstairs, Paddy races for the door of the living room where I've been writing. On the lowest shelf of the bookcase are his toys, and he brings them all to me, two and three at a time. I pick the green ball and we play fetch for a while. You can't outplay him—that's impossible—so instead I try to get him to where he won't be brokenhearted when I turn back to finish writing. Used to this, he lies on the floor next to me, ripping at what used to be a duck and is now simply his favorite broken object. The chomp of the plastic-lined wing is a sturdy, friendly sound.

Lala, meanwhile, is still asleep. She doesn't wake to the noise of Paddy jumping and hurling himself at the ball, and I'm glad.

She gets to sleep in because she's currently not working.

Yep. She lost her job.

And I'm *glad* she lost it.

This is so unlike the old me I hardly recognize myself.

The truth is, she hated her job. Okay, she liked the work well enough, and she liked the people. They liked her back, and she'd gotten the best review of her life a month before they let her go due to lack of projects (she was their last remaining contractor, and they'd kept her as long as they could).

But with the heat of a million suns, she hated getting up at five in the morning to overlap for a few hours with her Chicago office. It was necessary, but it was so hard on her that it affected all other parts of her life. She's a natural night owl, and given her druthers, she'd go to bed at one in the morning and get up at ten.

She works in tech, so losing a job isn't uncommon. After losing her job during the great recession, she'd been out of work for two years, during which I'd gone into full panic mode (always a good time for everyone). Normally, when she tells me a job has ended, my smile wobbles sturdily enough until I can hide somewhere to cry in terror for a while.

This time, though, when she told me, I felt a tiny red burst of fear followed by a walloping dose of *Okay, it'll be fine.*

We still have the house money in the bank. It might not be a *huge* amount of money to some, but it is to us. And it's more than we've ever had before. It's enough that I'm not worried about imminent eviction because of her job loss.

Also, according to our bank statements, we spend forty-two percent less than we did in the States. I'm not sure how that works, honestly. I don't feel as if we've cut back on things, and I *know* we spend more on groceries and takeout. Is it that we're simply less consumer-driven here? Amazon can't hurtle things into our hands at the speed we think of them. Honestly, it's a relief to not have a one-click button. Knowing that our cost of living is lower here helps keep my fear away.

More importantly, I have a bit more chill now, thanks to recovery and a meditation practice that works for me. So, as the one who manages our finances, I told her to take this whole month off. She agreed only after checking to see that my Venice-shaped birthmark was still in the right place, verifying that I was, indeed, her actual wife and not a pod-person replacement.

Now, as I journal, as Paddy chomps the dead duck, Lala sleeps.

I have some yogurt and muesli before heading to my (thankfully viewless) desk to work. Tuesday mornings are dedicated to making question and answer videos for my students in my 90 Days to Done writing classes. I forget my camera is on, and in my mind's eye, I can see each student in front of me as I speak. Paddy sits behind me on my office couch, making a guest appearance now and then.

After I finish recording, and before I grab another cup of tea, I quit the community choir.

Which is annoying.

A couple of weeks ago, we joined the community choir that a friend belongs to. We wanted to make some new friends, and while singing is really my thing, Lala was game to come along. But while it's been fun, I've been having hummingbird-like heart palpitations because of the way people incorrectly wear their masks. Singing is still a high-risk activity, and the choir director likes to bunch us up so close our shoulders brush. The BA5 strain of Covid-19, combined with the fact that very soon I'm keynoting a writing conference and traveling internationally, has made me decide to quit.

I hate quitting.

But I know I'd hate getting Covid more, and Lala agrees with me.

Minutes after sending the email of quittitude, the choir director responds. "I have to say I think you're making a huge mistake leaving the choir. Backing off from anything that challenges your anxiety is weak. It simply feeds that anxiety."

I can see her point, and if I were retreating into my house to never leave it again, this might be fair. But I'm choosing to lower my risk in order to engage in activities that have a higher value for me, and this email makes my head hurt. My email to her was both friendly and apologetic. I even sent along my best knee-slapper, because I'd been in charge of bringing the joke of the week. (What do you call a pretty girl on a banjo player's arm? A tattoo! Lala, who plays the banjo, has a tattoo of a gorgeous fat cowgirl on her arm, so this joke is also true!)

But the choir director says only that I'm making a huge

mistake. In real life, she has an enormous personality and terrifies me. In email, apparently, she has no bedside manner. My dander up, I write another email back, detailing exactly what I'm feeling and why it's okay that I'm making this choice. Lala is now awake, and before I send it, she talks me down. "You don't need to convince her of anything. You can take out that line. And that one."

So, still violently hating being a quitter but honestly relieved we don't have to practice that terrible George Michael medley anymore, I confirm the quitting by sending the last, now-much-shorter email.

With the kettle heating for yet more tea (is this my fourth cup now? Fifth?) I hide Paddy's ball in the living room while he waits in the kitchen. As he searches for it, roaring up and over our new couch like it's his, his rapture is enough to ease my guilt over quitting, and by the time I take my tea back to my desk, there's a new email waiting from someone I've been dying to hear from.

My editor.

She's had my newest novel for two weeks, and here it is: her verdict. I'm about to open her editing letter.

Getting an editing letter is like finding out your grade in the most important class you've ever taken. Except it's never an *A*. That's as it should be—your grade should never be an *A*. All books need revision. But will it be a *B*? Or was this a swing and a miss, a big fat *F*? Perhaps she'll say that rather than embarking into this new genre (paranormal women's fiction) I'd be better suited to going back to writing thrillers or romance. Or digging ditches, maybe.

I slap at the mouse, fumbling as I open the attachment.

Theresa's letter starts, "This is the best thing I've ever read from you. Like, hands down the best. You were always very good. This book might be great."

I would cry if I weren't so giddy. I might be levitating. I'm not sure.

I've worked with this editor on five books before this one, and she's even read a few of my books that she wasn't hired to edit. In fact, before I got an agent, before my first book was bought by HarperCollins, Theresa read a sample chapter of my first novel that I'd entered in a competition. She left me a comment on Ravelry, a knitting social media site. "You're a strong writer," she'd said to me way back in 2007. "You will be published." She was the first person in the publishing industry who believed in me. Over the course of my career, I've worked with a lot of developmental editors, but hands down, she's been the best one, the one from whom I've learned the most. When she flags something that needs strengthening, she gives the why behind it. She's an incredible writing teacher as well as a fantastic editor.

And I know this: she doesn't blow smoke. She's always kind, but she doesn't pull punches.

So I can trust her when she says it's hands down the best thing she's read from me.

Paddy noses my knee. He gives me the mournful spaniel look which is his way of showing great joy.

"You're right." I hiccup. "I am really happy."

I spend the rest of my workday doing work things, editing students' writing, running a write-in on Zoom, trying to swallow back enough of my joy that I don't float out of my chair and bob around at the ceiling, an untethered helium balloon of delight.

When I'm as done with work as I can be, I open the door to our small storage room where we keep things like Lala's bike, and extra chairs for parties we hope we get to have someday. I have three boxes stored in here, mostly photo albums and miscellaneous things that might come in handy. In one of them is our border collie's leash (RIP darling Clara), and I've been meaning to get it out. Paddy's strong pulling is helpful for going up hills, but even in the best of circumstances, holding onto his leash strains my back and neck.

But Clara's hands-free cross-body lead, when I find it, will be perfect.

Okay, it's not in this box.

Not in this one either.

Ah. Here it is, right on top of box number three. Fabulous! How clever I am for bringing it, the only dog thing I chose to ship over.

In my fingers, it feels a little clammy.

Shit.

Is it damp? Really? I hold it to my nose.

Yep. The scent of mildew makes my stomach tighten.

We run a dehumidifier all the time. It pulls one to two liters of water from the air a day. The storage room, though, is behind a closed door. I'd been crossing my fingers that things weren't wet in the boxes out there, which I can now see was foolish in Wellington's maritime climate.

But the damp will have to be a problem for another day because I have a leash in my hand, and while Lala told me she took Paddy for a walk earlier, he's clearly forgotten that he's ever been on a walk in his whole life.

So we go out. Carefully, we pick our way down the slippery, uneven steps.

The bluster of the storm has blown itself out and even though I've brought my magnificent rain hat with me, I don't think I'll need it. We aim ourselves toward Paddy's favorite hill, but where we'd normally turn right, the hill has washed itself away in a rather spectacular manner, the mud almost all the way across the road.

Quite casually, Wellingtonians call these mudslides "slips." They happen often here in our hilly city, and the entire road is closed to both directions of traffic. To Paddy's dismay, we can't go up the hill where he'd like best of all to go. I'm not as upset, though. This means I'm off the hook for hoofing it up the mountain.

Which way then?

If I go left, down this way and around the cattery (will we ever get used to this hilarious word?), then I'll connect with a road that winds through the trees and back up around Wadestown. We'll come out near the dairy, then we'll have a nice tromp through the village on our way back to Paddy's house.

Paddy likes this choice of direction too.

We greet Bella, a small staffie puppy that lives nearby. Someday I'll get Bella's owner's name, but does a person's name really matter when they're leading a black and white puppy around? Not so much. I wouldn't expect anyone to talk to me either, with that much frantic cuteness jumping at my feet.

The late afternoon sunlight is glorious, a clear winter light that tastes of hope and ozone. As we start up Paddy's street, he finally stops pulling as hard, perhaps aware that his fun time is almost over.

And look! At the base of April and Jules's walkway, there's been another slip! I twist sideways to fit past the mud and greenery to go up their raised path. It's not a bad one, less than five feet high, and there's nothing above it that would be threatened if the slip got bigger. But it makes me think again that when we buy a house in New Zealand, perhaps we shouldn't buy one on a hill. Of course, in

Wellington, that's like trying to buy a house not near a geological fault. With *seven* faults running through Wellington, that's almost as impossible as finding a house on flat land.

I creak open the gate, popping Paddy into his yard. He races into the empty house through the dog door, going all the way through to the front room so he can stare balefully out the window, reminding me of how it feels to leave a dog behind. This once-a-week dog works out well in so many ways. I only feel guilty every seven days instead of every time I leave the house.

I walk home with the Rebel Author podcast to keep me company, and when I get there, Lala's immersed in her online drawing class, so I do the most luxurious thing in the world—I get into the tub while it's still light out.

A few weeks ago, I turned fifty to very little fanfare. I worked all day, then we went to our first choir practice (in retrospect, we should have gone to a fancy dinner). But in the mail, I got a huge box so gorgeously fragrant I knew what was in it even before I opened it.

Lush bath bombs, sent by my sister Bethany. Lush makes the best bath stuff in the world, and I love their bubble bath bars. As mentioned, I'm cheap, so usually I buy myself one bar of bubble bath at a time, and instead of dropping the whole thing in, I break it into pieces. I can often get seven or eight baths from a single bar. And in this box? There are *so* many bombs and bars. A lifetime of them, if I were to break them into my normal small pieces.

So today I splurge, using an oxymoronic whole half. I light a birthday candle that my goddaughter sent me and slip into the bubbles. I scroll TikTok for a while, then I read the thriller I'm immersed in.

Lala knocks on the stained-glass window just above me.

I jump, splashing. The house is oddly constructed, and the front foyer looks directly into the bathroom through this window. Since the front door is also glass, that means that if you're standing naked at the bathroom sink when NZ Post delivers your package, they get to see *your* package. It hasn't happened yet, but it's only a matter of time. "Hello, Creeper McCreeperson."

She leers in delight. "You ready for dinner?"

I'm starving, and she's serving her Moroccan chicken. "Getting out!"

It's full dark now, and the ferry from the South Island is chugging in, its white lights shining over the black waters. Dinner is delicious, and post walk and bath, I'm warm and floppy.

After dinner, we watch an episode of *The Witcher*. My eyes are heavy, and I know I only have an hour of TV in me before I'll need to toddle off to bed. I can't follow a damn thing in this second season—the politics of the show are beyond me, and I just don't care. I only watch because I like how Geralt looks from the back in those leather pants.

And it's just a good excuse to watch TV with Lala, which we sometimes forget to do. I love sitting on our new couch, cuddled against her, my knitting moving slowly in my hands, the light of the TV flickering in front of us. The heat pump has warmed the room, and my brain detaches from its perpetual need to work-work-work. I could stay like this forever.

But the scenery the characters are striding across—green, rolling hills, low dark mountains in the background—what does it remind me of?

Oh, yeah.

"Looks like New Zealand," I say.

She shakes her head. "It's shot in the UK."

It hits me then.

Today is the twenty-sixth of July.

Grabbing the remote, I sit up. I pause the show. "Guess what today is?"

Her eyes widen. "*Crap*. Wait, no, you just had your birthday. What day is it?"

"We almost forgot! It's our one-year anniversary of moving around the world."

"Oh," she says simply. "Happy anniversary."

And this is how we celebrate the thing we almost forgot about:

We smile at each other. We kiss.

Then I press play and melt against her side again. Soon I'll go to bed, and she'll probably do something like play a video game or draw. She'll come to bed long after I'm asleep.

Then I'll get up early and she'll sleep in because she doesn't have to get up at five anymore, and a new day, equally worthy of celebration, will start all over again.

Chapter 13

Blown Away

This is how I die, then. In an Airbnb. Huh. I wonder how the company will spin it. Will my demise affect its stock shares? Luckily for them, I'm in New Zealand, and the rest of the world doesn't really notice us down here, so it probably won't even make the news.

I cower under the covers, clutching my clenched fists against my chest, my eyes screwed shut. I've shoved earplugs so deeply into my ears that they hurt, but still the wind howls through my head. The bed shakes as if four strong men each have hold of a different leg and are trying to toss me out of it.

It's kind of interesting to know how I will die.

Kiwi-American author Rachael Herron died this week when the tiny house she was in was tossed off a cliff into the Tasman Sea.

It's not a bad way to go, is it? Terrifying, of course, but not actually embarrassing. Once, in college, I needed to blow my nose and all I could find was an old, used, shredded tissue at the bottom of my backpack. While inhaling in preparation to blow, I sucked half of the Kleenex into my esophagus, blocking my windpipe. Idiotically, I ran to the bathroom because I didn't want anyone to see me choke to death, and I stood watching myself go blue in the mirror as I attempted to wheeze around the now-soggy lump. *She died choking on a dirty Kleenex. That's what they'll say at the funeral.* My life didn't flash before my eyes —instead, I used those few seconds to imagine the shame this ignominious death would bring upon my family. Then someone came in, gave me a half-assed Heimlich, which shifted the tissue enough for me to grab a breath and cough it up, and I did not die, even though the lung infection I got from the incident almost made me wish I had.

Something large and heavy thumps against the wall, and I gasp, diving further under the blankets. Is this it? The tiny house *appeared* to be built into the ground, not resting on a trailer or wheels, as some tiny homes are, but what do I know? Not much, apparently—I didn't even know this storm was coming, but according to the dribble of reception I have on my phone, the winds are hitting eighty-five knots (a hundred mph) and rising. I make the classic mistake of looking up the Beaufort wind force scale. Eighty-five knots is well past hurricane force. Under the "Land Condition" notes for hurricane force, the scale simply reads *Devastation*.

Earlier today, I drove four hours north of Wellington to have a solo writing retreat (oh, those three magical little words) in the middle of nowhere on the west coast of the North Island. I was deep in cattle country, and I didn't understand any of the road signs selling things that apparently helped with milk production and bull virility. Without ever seeing my host, I parked at a farmhouse and transferred my suitcase and groceries into his four-wheel drive truck (they call them utes here, short for utility vehicle). In it, I traversed dirt roads toward the sea, opening and closing five gates, cursing the rain and mud every time I had to get out of the ute again. Fifteen minutes later, having bumped through myriad green and muddy paddocks, I reached the place they called the Nest.

My heart took flight. The tiny house was exactly as the pictures had shown—the outside bathtub overlooking nothing but grazing cows, emerald hills, and breaking waves. Two walls of the house were glass, made of multiple sliding glass doors. If I wanted, I could open those walls all the way up. Probably not in this weather, though.

I just needed to get my bags inside.

It's important to know that New Zealanders have a charming trust in humanity, and it's one of my favorite things about them. They don't put guardrails at the edges of glorious views, and if there does happen to be a warning sign in place, *you must heed it* because they *only* warn you of the most extreme and terrible ways to die. I once hiked down a trail that had a sign warning "Steep slope," and ended up—literally—swinging from tree branches to find my next foothold.

Here, the Nest had a small deck. No railing, of course. The lip of the deck dropped away over the edge of the cliff to the waves far below.

With no exaggeration, the wind gusted so hard as I went toward the door that I had to drop my suitcase and cling to a windowsill to prevent myself from being blown off the deck.

No problem. I've got this. I clawed the door unlocked, threw myself and my suitcase inside, and took a deep breath.

I had to make one more trip to the ute to get my grocery bags.

I could do it.

This is not Saipan. This is not 1986. This is not Supertyphoon Kim. As a teenager, I'd lived through a monster typhoon, and while evacuating our house, I'd watched my mother get picked up by the wind and thrown into a palm tree, breaking her ribs. Our neighbor had belly-crawled out of his house to drag her inside. I've struggled with a fear of wind ever since.

But this wasn't that.

This was a glorious four-day solo writing retreat.

I just had to get those last few bags in.

I stepped out of the Nest, losing my breath at the ferocity with which the wind slammed into my body. I clung again to the windowsills with my fingers, digging my nails into the wood as I made my way around the building to where I'd parked the ute.

Crap—the ute's bumper was flapping, and not gently. The wind was ripping the bumper off the vehicle, the thick plastic almost torn in half. I took a video of it thrashing in the gale to prove to the host that I hadn't chewed off his fender on purpose. Then, since this was definitely a Kiwi farm truck, and because I'm a Herron, I dug out of my bag the duct tape I was carrying, and with a few long pieces, taped the bumper back on. That helped, but the wind still yanked at it.

A memory rose: the eye of the typhoon going over Saipan, the terrible hour of sinister silence after nothing but chaos, Mom moving our Jeep from what had been the lee of the house to the other side that would be the new lee when the eye passed over, stubbornly insisting on doing it herself, even with her broken ribs. With that in mind, I reparked the farm's ute so that it was in the lee of the Nest.

Then I clawed my way back inside with my groceries, again managing not to be blown off the deck to my doom.

Safely inside, I unpacked. Of course I did. I put my clothes in the closet, and I spread my few toiletries on a washcloth next to the bathroom sink.

In the tiny kitchen, I unpacked my groceries. To my disappointment, there was no oven. Nor was there a microwave or air fryer or any way to heat anything other than the gas stovetop. I'd seen the stovetop in the pictures but hadn't thought to verify that an oven lived underneath it instead of the cabinet full of cups. I'd brought a whole chicken to cook, as well as a couple of meat pies. Those just wouldn't work as dinner without an oven.

But that was okay. It had to be, because I was *not* leaving this place, not while the storm raged. I was at least an hour away from the nearest convenience shop, ninety minutes from a grocery store. Night was already dropping, and the wind was getting louder, so I heated the kettle because I had an ace in the hole. For some reason, at the last minute during my shopping trip, I'd added a four-pack of ramen. I hadn't had instant ramen in years, but it would be dinner every night, apparently. That was fine. (In fact, it was delicious. Tom yum ramen, who knew?)

My goal while on retreat was to rest and think. I had an image of lighting the candles I'd brought and writing in my notebook for hours that first night, setting myself up for the rest of the weekend.

That didn't happen.

Instead, the sound of the wind rose in a never-ending crescendo.

I tried to release the tension in my jaw, attempting to

loosen the way my upper molars ground into my lower ones. I slept with a nighttime bite guard—did anyone ever wear those when they weren't sleeping? Should I try?

As the rain hammered sideways, water started to pour through the windward window, even though it was shut tight. I placed a bath towel along the sill and hoped it would be good enough.

I ate my ramen.

Full night had fallen, and the thing about a tiny home made mostly of windows was that with a light on inside, all I could see was myself. I quickly tired of looking at the frightened woman with the wild eyes, so I rolled down all the blinds and ate half a block of Whittaker's Creamy Caramel.

I read for a while, trying to ignore the way the room shook. There was no Wi-Fi, but surprisingly, there was just enough cell reception to be able to send video messages back and forth to Lala.

Holding up the phone, I said, "Listen." Would she be able to hear the roaring? The clattering?

A few minutes later, her reply straggled its way into my phone. "Oh, my god. That's intense. You sure you're okay?"

"I'm okay!" I chirped back. "Totally great! Hope the wind doesn't blow this box off the cliff!"

On the video response, her face was startled. "Sounds like you're in an airplane, actually. I'm sure that there have been other storms that little house has made it through, but *wow*. Sounds like a lot."

Hang on. She wasn't supposed to be alarmed. She was supposed to reassure me, didn't she know that? But I gamely responded, "I'm sure glad living in Wellington cured me of my fear of wind! I'm not scared *at all!*"

It was almost true. Living in Wellington had given me a *slightly* higher tolerance for wind. When it howled outside our house, I still grimaced but could enjoy looking out our window at the whipping trees. Sometimes the roof creaked and various things went bang in the night, but at home, I chose to call my rapid heartbeat a product of excitement, not anxiety. They feel the same, after all. In *Atlas of the Heart,* Brené Brown says, "Similar sensations are labeled 'anxiety' when we perceive them negatively and 'excitement' when we perceive them positively. One important strategy when we're in these feelings is to take a deep breath and try to determine whether we're feeling anxiety or excitement. Researchers found that labeling the emotion as excitement seems to hinge on interpreting the bodily sensations as positive. The labels are important because they help us know what to do next."

So at home, I could label my wind anxiety as excitement, and believe myself most of the time.

But in Wellington, the entire house didn't judder and shake continuously. Here at the Nest, the couch shook under me. The dining chairs at the table danced the same way. The silverware clattered in its drawer endlessly.

The noise and shaking didn't mean the house would blow away. Of course not. How often did you hear about that, anyway? Houses didn't *usually* blow over.

This one wouldn't blow away.

Right?

A few months ago, my cousin Bob came up from the South Island to spend the weekend with us. When we were kids, my sisters and I played on Uncle Jim's farm with Bob and his three brothers, sliding down the wool chute into lanolin-filled fleeces, fishing for trout in the river, and jumping over stiles in the sheep paddocks.

Over pizza, now-grown Bob caught us up on his brothers, including Matt, the one who'd taken over the farm when Uncle Jim wanted to slow down.

"He and his wife are the entrepreneurial sort, y'know? Moved the old drover's cottage to the top of a hill and rent it out on Airbnb now. Making a killing on it." He brought up the pictures, and it was stunning, a snug cottage overlooking the green vales below.

"We have to stay there some day," I said to Lala.

Bob said, "Funniest thing happened a couple of weeks ago. That big storm we had?"

We nodded–it had hit us too, causing multiple landslides in our neighborhood.

"A couple had rented it that night, and get this–they got so scared by the wind that they just took off! Three in the morning!" He chortled, his face creased in delight. "Imagine! They were that scared."

Lala laughed.

Being a person who *used* to be afraid of wind, I laughed even harder. "You're *kidding*. What were they thinking? Did they think the cottage would blow away? Where did they think they would go to? A place where the wind *wasn't* blowing? Can you even picture it? They're packing their stuff into the car in the wind and then running...where?" The more I thought about it, the funnier I thought it was. A nighttime terror, a scramble for the things they'd unpacked, a pell-mell drive through farmlands and dark, stormy roads. How silly! How hilarious!

Now, after I've eaten my ramen and failed to journal, I'm curled in the fetal position as the wind shakes the Nest. Who decided to call it that, anyway? Stupid name. Not only do nests blow out of trees *all the time*, but trees themselves blow over. Regularly.

Because the floorboards are shaking so much, the bed judders without ceasing. I moved it away from the wall shortly after crawling into the sheets, in case being against the wall was the cause of its violent motion, but it turns out the vibration is coming up through the floor. The wind is so loud that if someone were here with me, we'd have to shout at each other to be heard.

I'm angry at Bob for telling us the story of the tourists at Matt's cottage. And at myself, for thinking the story was hilarious. If Lala were here with me and if we'd never heard that story, I'm sure I would have already freaked out enough to talk her into leaving. *We'll go find a hotel somewhere. New Plymouth, maybe? We can't die this way.* We would have had to find our way through the paddocks and all the gates—we would have had to store the key in the barn and swap the duct-taped ute for our own car and then get on the road in the dark and rain, our hearts beating out of our chests the whole time.

But Lala's not here.

And I'd mocked the terror of those poor tourists.

So now I have to ~~die~~—I mean, stay here.

As the bed rocks more aggressively, I try to figure out my odds of survival. I have never heard of a tiny house blowing off a cliff. So that's good. And there have been storms here before. Also good. Using this cold logic, I give myself a seventy percent chance of making it through the night. The other thirty percent says I'll go over the cliff with the house, still wrapped in the bedsheets.

They aren't bad odds, honestly. So I should try to sleep.

I'm a terrible sleeper, though, even on the best of nights. With the slightest twinge of regret, I think of the bottle of wine the host left me in the little refrigerator. Alcohol isn't a temptation anymore, and I've had no serious thoughts about drinking it. That said, it *would* help me sleep. The consideration takes less than a second or two. It would help me sleep *and* give me a migraine. If I did make it through the night, tomorrow I'd have to reset my sobriety date. Ugh. Plus, one single bottle would just whet my appetite for another bottle or two tomorrow, and I'm clear about this: I'm not leaving this place until it's check-out time or until I'm tossed over the cliff, whichever comes first.

I think of home. Lala said the storm was raging there too, and I imagine our cozy, stable house. More than a hundred years old, nestled into an east-facing hill, *it* knew how to ride out a gale.

My neck aches. My jaw is exhausted. Even my fingers hurt from being clenched.

I *really* want to sleep.

It hits me then, the answer landing almost audibly in my mind: I only have one option.

I have to accept this storm, along with the fear.

Rolling over, I groan. *Gah.*

Stupid acceptance is the answer. Yet again. And it's so maddening that 1) it's such an easy solution and 2) it always takes me so long to remember that it's the answer.

Fine.

I whisper, "I accept."

My muscles are still rigid, and I realize that it's kind of like hissing, "I'm *fine*" when you're obviously not.

So I take a breath and try to melt my body into the bed.

I'm rewarded with a walloping gust that body slams the house like a furious wrestler. I'm shocked the windows don't blow in.

Another memory rises. *The storm boards have already*

ripped off like soggy cardboard. The hallway windows implode, dagger-like glass shards embedding themselves in the opposite wall mere seconds after Mom walks past them.

I shake my head to clear away the memory. This is not a supertyphoon, and I'm not a teenager. I claw the blankets off my head and stare into the darkness. I'm fifty years old, four years older than my mother was when she'd been picked up by the storm and flung into the tree. I don't have a husband off-island and three kids to protect. Good grief, I'm here on a *writing retreat* because I've built a life in which I get to do that. I've made this part of my job.

My worry suddenly strikes me as funny. Fear is like that sometimes, requiring only a subtle nudge to go from terrifying to ridiculous. In that moment, I can see myself clearly. I'm curled up in bed, a ball of rigidity instead of what I should be: a woman full of gratitude for this excitement, for this *gift*.

I laugh out loud and my entire nervous system relaxes.

Excitement, not anxiety. It feels the same.

It's my choice.

So I choose a train.

That's it—*that's* what this shaking feels like. Earlier I'd thought the juddering of the house felt like being on an airplane in turbulence, but that wasn't quite right. Turbulence comes with those stomach-churning drops, and this is more of a constant shaking side-to-side, no up and down.

It feels as if I'm lying in a sleeping car on a train. Not that I've been in a sleeping car (yet), but I can imagine it's just like this, loud and shuddering.

Tonight, I'll sleep on board the train as it chugs through miles and miles of dark countryside. It's exciting, this travel. And *quite* safe, I'm sure.

I close my eyes, feeling the rumble of the wheels below

me, hearing the clanks of the metal and wood as the carriage moves through space, carrying me with it.

In the morning, the wind still roars, but it's no longer dark and I'm alive and actually rather well-rested. Excitement flows easily, without even needing to push anxiety aside, and by ten a.m. I'm in the tub outside. I have to run the hot tap almost constantly as the wind cools the water like it's blowing on its coffee, and I do have one mortifying moment when two farmers *stroll across the paddock next to me,* but I send them a sharp "Hello, I see you but stay away" wave and remain well under the waterline.

When they're out of sight, I scamper inside and dry off. I open the sliding glass doors to the wind.

Then I write.

Chapter 14

Embarrassed Hobbits

When I scan my passport at the check-in kiosk at Wellington Airport, instead of printing out our boarding passes, the screen reads, "See attendant."

No worries. We have *plenty* of time. Even though Wellington is a small airport, we've still arrived two hours early for the flight to Auckland that will connect to our non-stop flight to San Francisco. It's our first visit back to the US since we emigrated fifteen months ago.

The attendant, a young woman with a friendly face, loses some of her smile as she pushes buttons. "Huh." She presses more keys. "This is weird," she says. "I don't understand this at all, but I'm kind of new. I hate to ask this, but is there any way you have a different passport?"

I nod. "I have a US passport, but it's expired. I'll just fly on my New Zealand passport today."

That doesn't seem to relieve her. "Can I see your US one, please?"

"I don't have it. I had to mail it in for replacement. It's been months, but I haven't gotten it back yet." I'm getting nervous. "This isn't, like, a real problem, right? I'll be able to get on the plane?"

"I, uh..." She raises a hand to hail a manager.

Mitch the manager arrives and clacks at the same keyboard.

Something flutters in my stomach as I ask again, "I *will* be able to get on the plane. Right?"

He squints into the screen, then his expression falls. "Maybe not. I'm thinking...no. You probably won't be able to get on the plane."

Shock flows through my veins, cold and sharp. "Pardon me?"

"Unfortunately, if you have a US passport, the US requires that you fly on it if entering or leaving the States."

Wait. They could do that? Just keep me out? What about the plane ticket I bought? And all our plans? Of all the things I've been stressing over for this trip, not being able to board the plane hasn't been one of them. "But...but I'm a dual citizen. What should it matter?"

Mitch shrugs. "It shouldn't. We certainly don't think it does. But to the US, it matters. We won't be able to let you on the plane. I'm sorry. The US requires other countries to enforce their rule at the place where you board. Not there, when you arrive."

"But why? Why is that?" I don't want to sound like a typical American, demanding answers that aren't her due, so I add, "I know it's not your fault. Thank you for helping me. Do you *happen* to know why that is?"

He slants a quick look at me, and I try to look extra-super-duper Kiwi. I'm not sure how to do that, so I just smile and keep my gaze directly fixed on him, hoping I look smart and kind, not as panicked as I'm starting to feel.

"Yes, actually." He glances over my shoulder and lowers

his voice. "If an American citizen arrives on American soil, border patrol can't legally deny them entrance. With or without a passport, your citizenship entitles you to entry. That's a boatload of paperwork for them, which they don't want. So we have to be the bad guys, not them."

Fuck. My brain frizzles with static, then I remember. "I have a photo of my passport. Would that help?"

"Maybe?"

I pull it up and shove my cell at him.

He examines it, then picks up his phone. "I'll try calling the Wellington American embassy."

With false cheer, I say to Lala, "Looks like you'll be having a three-week vacation in the States without me! Have a good time!"

Her eyes big, Lala holds up her crossed fingers. "I have hope," she says.

Me, on the other hand—something shameful warms my blood.

Relief.

I tuck the feeling back into my chest and try to pretend I don't imagine (just for a second) going back to our flat without Lala, three unplanned and blissfully solo weeks opening before me like a rolling green vista. I wouldn't have to go to any gatherings or have big dinner parties. In fact, I wouldn't have to see a single other person. I'd get groceries and sushi delivered. I'd leave the lights off and tiptoe at night so our neighbor downstairs wouldn't even come up to say hi. I'd be *alone.*

Even from three feet away, I hear that the woman Mitch is on the phone with is mighty unhappy. "Yeah," he says. "She said it's expired. I know. Yes. Yes." Finally, Mitch winces as if the woman has slapped him through the line. "I understand. Okay. Yes."

Then he bangs down the phone with a satisfied thump. "You can fly! Make sure you tell them in Auckland that Officer Herschel at the Wellington embassy granted you permission. And she is really *mad* at you."

Lala says, "Americans, am I right?"

He laughs, looking pleased. "Have a good trip."

I tell myself that the tacos will make it all worthwhile, pick up my backpack, and follow my wife toward the gate.

Eighteen hours later, we reach passport control. I wave Lala ahead. "I'll see you soon. Or maybe I won't! Write me while I'm in prison, won't you, darling?"

She doesn't think I'm funny.

Neither does the border control agent to whom I present myself. "I don't have my US passport with me."

He shakes his head. "You couldn't have gotten on the plane without your passport."

That's right, buddy. I'm not here, and you can't see me. "Would you like to look at my New Zealand passport?" No one had even checked it in New Zealand—I'd boarded both planes without showing a single piece of identification. Surely they'll want to see it here?

But he doesn't. He just shakes his head and says, "Follow me."

I end up in a section of the San Francisco airport I've never been in before, the area to which they shunt the problems. There aren't many of us. There are three men sitting separately and one woman and man sitting together. I'm ushered into my own row and warned not to take out my cell phone.

Four rows away, a border control agent is arguing in quiet Spanish with the couple. They're too far away for me to catch any words, but it's obvious they're upset as he stalks away from them.

Taking a breath, I prepare to wait as long this takes. Will there be a fine? If so, how big? Could they send me back, or was Mitch right when he said they have to let me enter?

But before I can really fire up my anxiety engines, a woman calls my name. I follow her to a tall desk. The woman asks me to explain myself.

As I do, I feel the eyes of the others on me. How long have they been waiting?

She clicks a few keys, and says, "Okay, then, off you go, follow the red line on the carpet to baggage claim."

"Excuse me?"

The look she gives me is sharp. "I can see your passport renewal's still making its way through the system. You're cleared to enter."

I gasp. All five people behind me are people of color. This is the mortifying *height* of white privilege. I take one last guilty look at the five people hunkering miserably in their chairs, and without showing a scrap of paperwork or ID to cross the American border, I enter.

Two days later, our party swirls around me.

I'm drowning.

The words and love and hugs are pulling me under, and I can't figure out how to swim up to the light and air. It's stupid, so very stupid, and the worst part is that I've done this to myself. I'd love to blame someone else. Anyone at all will do, and I do try, but I can't. This is on me. *I* chose this lovely big house in Oakland where we're staying, perfect for hosting. *I* sent out the email to forty of our closest friends inviting them to what I called an "open house." *I* planned every bit of this.

I called this gathering an open house because it wasn't supposed to be a party. The Airbnb rules stated clearly that we were not allowed to have one. Instead, this open house was supposed to be a cool, easy, mellow day during which people came and went. Two or three people would arrive, and we'd have an intimate chat, then they'd leave just as the next few people showed up. *Oh, lovely to see you! Must you go already? Well, look who's coming up the walk!*

But everyone arrived at once, because of course they did, and I'm about to chew off my own arm. Or my own leg. Or someone else's limb, I don't care at this point. Anxiety constricts my breath and sweat drips down my back.

I'm seated on the couch with two people I love, trying extremely hard to hear them over the cacophony of the voices of the twelve other people who are also shoved into the living room. I won't let anyone stand outside to talk, worried about the "no party" rule. I know the rule is probably to prevent frat parties, not to prevent a collection of forty- and fifty-year-olds from talking about abortion rights and the best new shows on Netflix before the sun has even set, but those claws of anxiety have dug into my very soul at this point. Honestly, I'm hoping that some people will get tired of the noise and leave.

But, of course, *I'm* the one who's tired of the noise and wants to flee. As the volume rises in the room, so does my agitation. My phone buzzes in my pocket. My little sister Bethany has been staying with us in an extra bedroom. She texts, *I've escaped to my room. Tell me if you need me.*

Need her? I need no one. There are altogether too many someones all around me, and I'm wildly jealous that my sister can disappear and I can't.

I catch my friend Sophie's gaze. She's worse with crowds than I am, but I'm on day five of socializing with no break, and the whites of her panicked eyes infect me. We turn into spooked horses, both of us straining to bolt. She, however, can collar her boyfriend and escape into a dark, quiet car. I have to stay inside the crush, stay in the room full of people I love, the people I want to urgently escape.

I take my thirty-thousandth deep breath and turn back to my friends, a bright smile lacquered to my face. *Help*, I whisper without moving my lips. *Help*.

At eight p.m., the stated ending time, I usher people out as lovingly as I can, citing a blooming headache, which isn't a lie. I'm in bed twenty minutes later. Lying on unfamiliar sheets that bunch and twist underneath me, I stare up at the ceiling fan and pant.

At the beginning, our plan for this trip had been sensible. I made a spreadsheet (okay, maybe a teensy red flag) with three slots on each day: morning, afternoon, evening (red flags number two, three, and four).

First, we offered the slots to our families. We chose a couple of days to travel to see my dad and stepmom, and once Lala's father and brother and my sisters had laid their claims on our time, we started to fill in the other slots. I chose times for three open houses.

I had planned to leave plenty of time open for rest and relaxation.

Now, here in Oakland, I face the truth: I have failed. Utterly.

When I open the Google sheet on my phone, which I do at least fifteen times a day, a low hum of dread washes through my blood. Because of this goddamn spreadsheet and the way I've fucked it up, my social stress has shot through the roof.

Introverts are like electric cars. They hum along, quiet and self-contained.

Extroverts, on the other hand, are gas-powered. You can hear them coming a mile away, and they need to stop frequently for gas and snacks and chats with the guy behind the counter.

Ambiverts, like me, are hybrids. They need to be fully fueled (give us some social interaction) and fully charged (give us ample alone time) to work in peak condition.

On this trip, I have disconnected the battery and chucked it right out the window as I scream down the highway, spraying gasoline from flame throwers like I'm a war boy from *Mad Max: Fury Road*.

I send an email canceling the second open house.

That leaves just one more coming up in five days, and I secretly hope no one will come.

Bethany's pickup smells of the fresh bagels she's just bought. "Let's go get you a coffee and then drive along the water." She's the driving sister, the one who's explored the United States multiple times by herself, the one who, when stressed, gets in her truck and just *goes*. Driving with her is its own kind of magic. There's never any rush. We pull over whenever we feel like it and read every historical marker that catches our interest.

Talk comes as easy as the miles unroll, and the tightly wound ribbon in my chest unspools. She drives around the Emeryville Marina, and we admire the brightly painted boats and the earnest-looking joggers. I used to be a runner, so I assume they're probably having fun huffing and puffing, but there's no way they're having as much of a good time as I am, sitting next to my sister with no goal except to grill her about the accompanist we're going to sing with.

An accompanist! This will be a new thing for us.

We three Herron girls have good singing voices. When they're combined in winding harmony, they're gorgeous. But apart from at music festivals, karaoke bars, and at our mother's bedside while she was dying, we haven't sung together as adults. We always *mean* to, but we never do.

This time is different. Hiring the guitarist was Bethany's idea, and middle-sister Christy found one and snagged a spot on the calendar.

But I have concerns.

Some random dude, hanging out with us while we sing? I ask, "Who is this guy? Like, is he a guitar teacher, used to accompanying kids at recitals? Or is he more like a singer-songwriter?"

Bethany palms the wheel at the end of the marina, smoothly turning the truck. "I think he's more the latter."

"Oh, *god.* Is he going to want us to listen to him? Like, to his songs?"

She's firm. "No."

"But—he knows he doesn't get to sing, right? Did she tell him that?"

Bethany says, "He might want to sing."

"But he doesn't *get* to sing. This is for *us.*"

"Dude. Chill. He's the guy we hired to help us out. We're the boss. We call the shots."

We drive past two short men carrying long fishing rods. "Damn straight. We're in charge."

The clutch squeaks as we pull up to a light near the freeway entrance.

Without thinking, I say, "I just don't want to have to perform. For a man."

"Jesus. Why *would* you?" Bethany sounds horrified.

Startled, I hear the words I've just said. "I guess something in me automatically wants to please a guy, even if I don't give a shit who he is. Patriarchy, you know?"

"No. I do not know." Out of the three of us, Bethany is the one who gives the fewest shits.

"What if he compliments us or something?" I slide lower in the bucket seat. "Ugh. I'm going to want to suck in my stomach and sing pretty. I know I am."

As if I've handed her a personal challenge, Bethany says, "If he compliments us, I'm going to push out my stomach as far as I can *and* sing all the wrong notes on purpose."

I worship her. And I know I'll probably still suck in my stomach.

A few days later, Lala and I have a rare two hours to ourselves one morning before I'm scheduled to meet friends for lunch, so in this small pocket of found time, we go to our favorite coffee shop, the one we walked to a million times when we were first in love. How many times have we walked these streets, pulled along by a dog or two? Some houses have been repainted since we last passed by, and a gigantic mansion we've always admired is being gutted. We stop and watch the workers carrying out wooden beams and broken tiles. As they throw the detritus into a junk truck, the crashing sounds soothe my soul.

I lace my fingers again with Lala's, enjoying this moment of being together, no socializing necessary.

I've been so cranky with her on this trip, but this moment—this one is nice.

At the cafe, we sit outside in the perfect autumn weather. We people-watch and comment on passing dogs and cute babies. Everyone moves faster on their feet here than they do in New Zealand, dodging and weaving around each other at full speed. How is it only fifteen months since we lived here? It feels like either a few days or twenty years, but fifteen months makes no sense at all.

My mocha is strong, and my morning bun is covered with sugar. I relax and lose track of myself in the ease of the moment. For a second, I forget where I am, thinking I'm back home in Wellington, and I know this because I see a man in the crosswalk who resembles a friend. I'm about to say, *Hey, look, doesn't that guy look like Max in Oakland?* when I realize that the reason that dude looks like Max in Oakland is because he *is* Max in Oakland, crossing the street with his wife Kat. Saying nothing to Lala, I leap from my chair and stand at the edge of the crosswalk, my arms open wide. I can see their brains making a similar calculation: *That woman looks like Rachael, but she lives in New Zealand. Isn't that weird?*

Then there are hugs, lots of them, and we have a quick, delightful catch up. They only have fifteen minutes to spare, but they're glorious minutes, and we make them count. Lala and Max talk music, and Kat and I talk podcasts.

Then Kat says, "Be honest. Like, wherever we go, we take ourselves. Right? New Zealand isn't *actually* an easier place to live. Is it?"

Wincing, I tell her the truth. "It's easier."

She slaps the metal table. "Goddammit. I fucking *knew* it."

As we're saying our goodbyes, Max says, "You know, we should..." He trails off.

The spreadsheet flashes behind my eyelids. I feel my blood pressure spike, but I can see *him* perusing his own mental calendar.

He smiles and opens his arms for one last hug. "God, it's good to see you both."

On our walk back to the Airbnb, I say, "I'm *so* glad we got to see them. I can't believe we left them off the open house invite list."

Lala is horrified. "You forgot them?"

I puff out a breath. "We went over the invite list together! You were supposed to add people that I left off if you wanted to see them."

"Are you serious? I just thought you'd invite *all* our friends."

Oh, my god. No. We weren't getting married. Nor were we throwing the bon-voyage party of the century. That had been fifteen months before, and I was still emotionally scarred from saying goodbye to that many people.

So I break it down for her, shocked we've been on such separate pages. "First tier: family and best-best friends. They get time on the spreadsheet. Second tier, very close friends, like best friends, yes, but not *best*-best—"

Lala rolls her eyes.

I keep going. "Like, we love them with all our hearts, and we want to see them at the open houses, but unfortunately, as much as we hate the fact, they don't get a slot on the spreadsheet all to themselves because we don't have that much time in the country. Third tier is the people we'd love to see but don't really still connect with on a weekly, or even on a monthly basis. Those are the ones I didn't invite or forgot entirely. When was the last time you WhatsApped Max? Or Zoomed with him and Kat?" Even though the three of them have been in bands together, the answer is never. I know that.

Stubbornly, Lala says, "You should have invited all our friends to the open houses."

I drop her hand and walk faster, leaving her behind me. Over my shoulder, I spit, "*You* could have done that. But you didn't."

We attend a (best-best) friend's birthday party. The invite preview says it's a costume party and gives the date and time. Of course, because Julie is one of my closest friends, I don't actually *open* the Evite. I know where she lives. I text her that we're coming.

And so, because I don't click through, I don't learn that the costume party has a theme.

Or that the theme is 1920s Paris.

Until we arrive as hobbits.

Oops.

I go as a traditional hobbit, with a bit of harfoot thrown in, because I want the twigs-in-my-hair look. I know the difference between harfoots (harfeet?) and hobbits because Christy, a passionate *Lord of the Rings* fan, made a hobbit lookbook for us when we said we wanted to dress up. I'm wearing surprisingly comfortable slippers that look like big stuffed bare feet with hair on the toes, a green velvet cloak, and a vest I got at the thrift store. I've twisted flowers and twigs into my hair, and I like the look so much I wonder if I can get away with it on a normal day.

Lala, on the other hand, goes as a modern hobbit in winter, which I need to explain.

In all seasons in New Zealand, people go barefoot everywhere: buses, grocery stores, the library. (I'm convinced it's one of the reasons "be a tidy Kiwi" is a literal national catchphrase. After all, if people are often barefoot, broken glass on a sidewalk gets swept up immediately.) Even in winter, people still go barefoot, Kiwi dudes especially. It might be raining in midwinter, but you'll still see manly men sporting bare feet and naked legs. Their only concession to the weather is a puffer jacket over their shorts.

So at the party, Lala wears my greenstone necklace, a pair of the barefoot-hairy-toed slippers, shorts, and a puffer jacket. This is funny to absolutely no one else, but we find it *hilarious*.

We arrive early. Julie is charmed by our costumes, but Lala is mortified that I didn't read the invite. "Nineteen twenties?" she hisses as we help ourselves to drinks. "*Paris*?"

I grimace and offer, "Maybe we're French hobbits?"

Because I know I'll want to make an early exit, I commandeer the back sitting area, the one under the trees with a view of the hills. I drag my closest friends back there with us, and as night falls, I feel almost no guilt that we're at Julie's party, but not quite of it. The people around me are *my* people.

But even with my loved ones, a tension rises in my chest. And when a lull drops over us, the conversation grinding just a touch as we shift between gears, my heart pounds and again I feel like I'm drowning, the pressure building in my lungs—I need to breathe, but I can't, not here. If I were somewhere else, if I were home, then I could breathe again. I *think* I could.

Behind me, I hear other partygoers traipsing down the

shell-lined path. Their feet pause as they look at us, then I hear the scrape as they turn and head back to the main gathering. Perhaps they're other overwhelmed, socially awkward people, but I don't care. We got these chairs first. I don't turn around to look.

One day, plans get canceled, and I'm so happy I feel like a dog released on a beach to chase seagulls. Lala and I go into San Francisco to see the Guo Pei exhibit at the Legion of Honor.

I grin at her. "Just us. You and me."

She says, "Do you like me again?"

"No," I exclaim too quickly, knowing what a bear I've been. "I *love* you again."

She laughs, but there's pain behind her blue eyes that she can't quite hide, a hurt that says she'd expected me to protest, to say I didn't know what she was talking about. Instead, I'd upped the ante.

But I make it up to her by driving us to get the one food item we've been pining most for. The mission burrito we get at Taqueria Cancún pretty much makes up for everything—for me being a stressed-out jerk, for me overfilling the calendar, for me failing to breathe.

The burrito is perfect, grilled lightly, stuffed with rice and beans and cheese and salsa and half an avocado. It's ecstasy in a tube. We should have started our trip here.

Now, my sisters and I are singing together in Christy's backyard, and I'm trying not to cry.

We sing "Closer to Fine," by the Indigo Girls. I remember long, long ago, when I was falling asleep in my tent at a music festival, I heard two women singing it at a nearby campsite. Their harmonies drifted through the night so perfectly I could feel them crackle against my skin. The next morning, I found out Christy had been the one singing the harmony line, and I wished so badly that I hadn't gone to bed early and missed it.

Now, we're here together, and the song sounds better than I've ever heard it, even from the Indigo Girls.

Then Christy and Bethany sing rings around the Beatles as they do "You're Going to Lose That Girl." I fake my way through "Neon Moon" by Kacey Musgraves as Bethany leads, and when Chance, the accompanist (who is *darling* and nothing like the Sensitive Songwriter Dude I'd worried about) mentions "I Will Follow You into the Dark," he and I sing a version that would make a Death Cab for Cutie fan throw black roses onstage.

All told, we sing more than twenty songs together, and all of them (I swear to you) sound good. But nothing sounds as lovely to my ears as Woody Guthrie's "California Stars" recorded by Wilco and Billy Bragg.

Our little mama loved that song. It has the power to make me cry when I *think* of it, so it's no surprise that I well up as soon as we start singing it. But it's the way we sing it that moves me so deeply that I can hardly breathe, but not in the drowning way. More like the flying way.

Our voices wind around each other under the trees, taking turns. I'm the high harmony, then I move to the lead as one of them—I can't tell which—expertly takes the high notes from me. Then I'm the low harmony as Bethany (or maybe Christy) takes lead and Christy (or maybe Bethany) goes high.

And while I've sung along to the song a million times, I realize I've never listened to the words.

As we sing about dreaming on the bed of California stars, the deep, lovely longing of the words fills me, and I start to cry in earnest. My throat is tight and aching, but it doesn't matter, I'm somehow still mostly on pitch, and I'm still here, in this yard in the fog-laced sunshine, with my sisters, singing.

Here.

Together.

When I moved away from them last year, I thought I might die of grief. Stepping into the total unknown and leaving them behind was agony.

I know that this time, when we leave, it will hurt a tiny bit less, because this time, unlike last time, we'll be going *home*, to a place we love.

But in this exact moment, with Christy's dog Iris running around our feet and our harmonies merging in the air like magical spells cast with our breath, I am home in a way I can be nowhere else.

When we fly back to New Zealand, I use my New Zealand passport to board the Air New Zealand plane (take *that*, America). The eastbound flight is longer, and neither of us really sleeps on the red-eye. In Auckland, we miss our connecting flight, but we're both too tired to care. While we wait for the next one, we get breakfast and sit outside with looks on our faces as glazed as our donuts. I wonder where those other five people are now, the ones who were in the holding area at San Francisco International with me. I wonder if they're close to home.

Then we're on the plane to Wellington. It's a short, one-hour flight, and my heart keeps singing *almost-there-almost-there-almost-there.*

I have this thing I do when a plane is landing. When I think the wheels are just about to touch the tarmac, I take a deep breath. I hold it until the wheels make contact with the earth, then I slowly exhale as the brakes engage. By doing this, I have a job, and therefore, I don't care if the plane slams around or skids sideways. I simply have to breathe.

The plane touches down. In a small miracle, it's not windy today, and the landing is smooth. Our car is in the long-term lot, and while I know I'll spend the next few days embarrassed every time I flick on the windshield wipers instead of the blinker, I also know that even with stopping to collect our luggage, we'll be home in thirty minutes.

I lean against Lala's shoulder as the plane taxis toward the terminal. Finally, I exhale.

Chapter 15

In Which We Tramp

Merisha is one of those beautiful outdoorsy types, her hair long and curly and still wet from her shower or, more likely, from a swim with her favorite pod of dolphins. I have no doubt that at some point today she'll reach up one-handed and tie her hair into a charming topknot while, with the other hand, she'll fillet the trout she's just caught after abseiling into a grotto somewhere.

Her smile is bright, and she seems honestly thrilled to tell us about the seventy-kilometer hike Lala and I are about to embark upon. As we sit with her at a picnic table on a cloudy day in Mārahau, right at the top of New Zealand's South Island, she spreads out the map. "So, where are you visiting from?"

I know what people mean when they ask this after hearing our accents. I want to tell everyone we meet, "I'm half-Kiwi, really. I swear I am," but I've mostly stopped doing this. Because there were no tourists in New Zealand for so long, no one was treating us like visitors. But recently, more than two years after the pandemic started, New Zealand opened back up, and now we get asked it all the time. Last week, when I ordered a cappuccino, the barista slowly and carefully explained to me the different ways I could pay. I whipped out my local bank card and tapped the reader with it, saying, "Paywave is fine." I felt like *accidentally* dropping my Wellington Snapper bus card onto the counter too.

Now, I stammer to Merisha, "We're from Wellington." I let a beat go by. "Um, originally from the San Francisco area, though." Is that the right answer, the one I want to give? I think so—it explains our accents but also firmly claims our new hometown.

She grins. "I grew up in Wellington! You'll be ready for our hills, then."

We puff with pride that is yet unearned, then we listen intently as she points out places on the map. "Here you'll want to follow signs to the stream, not to the gulley. And over here, take a left, because if you take a right, you'll add an hour's hike to your day."

"Mmmm," we murmur. I'm trying to memorize everything she's saying, but Lala is swaying a bit, still dopey from the antinausea pill she took yesterday for the ferry crossing.

"And here, in the middle of the second day, you'll go inland for a bit. Make sure you eat a big snack here because there's a wee hill afterward."

My stomach clenches with sudden nerves. Anytime a Kiwi puts the word "wee" in front of anything, you can be sure it's the very opposite of small. "Got it," I say, not at all sure I have it.

She taps the map again. "On the fifth day, you can cross the tidal inlet after 12:57 but no later than 3:57 or the water will be too deep to be safe. If you turn to your right afterward, there's a foot wash if you want to clean off your water shoes. It's hidden off the trail a ways, so I always like to mention it."

I nod. Should I be taking notes? We have a printout of the itinerary, which I've almost memorized now, but all these little extra details seem important.

When Merisha's done and folding up her map, Lala says out loud what I've been thinking. "This is an overview, right? We'll get briefed again each day before we leave?"

Merisha's eyebrows rise. "Oh! This was your only overview. You'll just get a lunch from wherever you're staying. Easy as, though. You've got this."

Oh, no. We *should* have been taking notes.

Today, we'll hike thirteen kilometers, which I'm hoping we can do in four hours. Honestly, I'm looking forward to it. Time to think, time to ponder. It'll be meditative, our hiking poles swinging at our sides as we tramp through the bush.

And we have a lot to think about.

Thirteen days ago, we suddenly and unexpectedly got bank approval for a mortgage.

Banks here are much stricter than in the States, and while we were under consideration, they queried why I spent five dollars every Sunday (a charitable donation to my recovery meeting) and asked if I'd continue taking guitar lessons after we moved (thirty dollars every other week). We were only testing the waters, really. Our flat's lease is up in two months, and while we were almost certain we wouldn't get approved for a mortgage, at least we'd learn a little about the housing market. Surely that would help when we were truly ready to look for a house.

Then, less than two weeks ago, *the bank approved us.*

And seven days ago, after viewing two dozen properties in a whirlwind of open homes and private viewings, we saw the house of our dreams. Within an hour of viewing it, we offered on it. Thirty minutes later, the sellers agreed to the offer.

And yesterday, a mere twelve days after a bank approval we never expected to get, we went unconditional on the contract, which meant that the house was legally ours. So just a couple of weeks before our lease ends, we'll be living in our very own home in Wellington.

We're both still spinning, dizzy from the speed and joy and—on my part, anyway—abject terror that comes with making a major life decision. This, however, is how Lala and I have always worked. Get married? Sure! Buy a house? Why not? Lala never even saw the inside of our California home before we got the keys—unable to take time off work to view the property, she'd only seen the listing's photos and had trusted me enough to go along with it. Sell that house and make an international move? Boom, five months later, done. Why *not* buy a house in thirteen days?

Over the next five days of walking, we'll have a lot to think about. I can't wait to get out there.

Merisha hands us our lunches, we use the restroom, and we're off.

Only, not so much.

Seven hundred meters down the road, before we even get on the official trail, there's a cafe. Poor drugged Lala wants a last-chance coffee, and I can't blame her.

Twenty minutes later, we're underway again.

We have to stop, of course, to take a selfie under the trail entrance.

Then we walk a little farther.

Even though it's overcast and dripping, it's so warm that neither of us wants to wear our jackets and hats.

So we stop and rearrange our day packs.

More sunscreen is needed (the lack of pollution and thinness of the ozone layer mean we don't fuck around with SPF). This takes a while.

We walk a few more minutes, watching the birds and insects with interest, until those insects start gnawing at us. Sandflies! Which are as legendarily stupid and painful as everyone said they'd be.

So we make another stop to dig out the repellent and apply. I'm grumpy and snappish, and we're not even an hour into our hike. I want to *move*, to *go*. Not this constant stop-start-stop.

But then shoes need loosening (hers) and others need tightening (mine).

And do we really *need* pictures of every turn of the trail? Yes, it's green and lush, spiderwebs dripping with sparkles, and the sun is threatening to come out at any minute, but I'm pretty sure we won't know this green photo from any of the later green ones. But Lala wants pictures, so I grit my teeth.

A few minutes later, Lala realizes her hydration pack isn't connected to the mouthpiece.

"Sorry," she says. She's said it every time we've stopped.

I start to snap again, but I remember: this isn't a race. What am I *doing*? We're realizing a life's dream, to hike one of New Zealand's Great Walks. We're here together. We just bought a freaking *house*.

I take a deep breath. "There's no hurry."

She looks miserable as she fishes in the bottom of her backpack. "*You're* in a hurry, though."

"No. Take all the time you want. Seriously." Finally, I really do mean it.

I see her face relax just as the sun burns through the last of the clouds.

We hike the first hill and congratulate ourselves on our Wellington hill training. Then we take a nice long breather at the top.

That night, we stay in Anchorage, a long, white, sandy beach surrounded by bright blue water. The travel company has set up our tent, and it's huge—two cots with real blankets and pillows, an antechamber with Adirondack chairs, and an awning. We have about an hour before dinner, so we drop our packs and change into our swimsuits (called togs in New Zealand, something we now say because it's objectively just more fun to say togs).

The sand is powder soft, and the water is strangely both cool and warm. I float on my back, staring up into the blue sky. We have *walked* here. It took four and a half hours, which isn't that bad at all, considering that last "wee" hill before the track wound sharply downhill into camp. Overhead, three kākā tumble raucously through the air, and I feel, rather than see, a school of fish zoom past my ankles. When I rise from the water, I am as clean as salt.

Zeke, the travel company's sole employee at the camp, cooks us dinner. He makes spectacularly unremarkable fish, adequate salad, and very good potatoes, which is about exactly what I'd expect from a twenty-one-year-old guy majoring in adventure tourism. We are ravenous, and I eat two helpings of everything.

Overhead, my friend Orion is upside down, his skirt over his head.

And as we bed down into our separate cots, too tired to figure out how to push them together, my brain, which has been relatively quiet since I told Lala (and myself) that we were in no hurry, whirs to life. Lala goes to sleep instantly, which I would attribute to the hike, but it's what she does every night.

Two hours later, I'm still trying and failing to read myself to sleep, which is what *I* do every night. I'm anxious about everything: about the house and the mortgage and the rain that might roll in tomorrow. My mind races as if I've overheated it, and I can't cool it down.

Tomorrow we're supposed to hike nineteen kilometers, which will be farther than anything we've trained for. The tour company said we should be "comfortable walking for four hours," which we are. But tomorrow promises to be closer to a seven-hour hike. Maybe even eight, the way we stop. And we've never trained back-to-back long hikes. We've also never carried this much water in our backpacks. The company told us there would be fresh water along the trail, but there isn't—there's a boil-water advisory instead, and I'm worried that three liters each won't be enough to get us through a hot, seven-plus-hour hike.

The irritation I feel in my brain feels like the sand at the bottom of my bedding: scratchy, annoying, and all my fault.

Fucking *Kiwis*. They're so *hardy*.

At home, Lala and I regularly curse at them under our breath when we're out for a hike. We huff and puff our way up a hill, and no matter how steep the climb, we're always passed by jovial ninety-year-olds sprinting toward the summit, not the slightest bit sweaty. They chirp, "Good day for it, eh?" and we wheeze back, "Mgnnnnghhh."

On this longest day of our hike, I'm still nervous. It will be a hilly day, and worse, it promises to be a warm one too. We trained in winter, so this is another thing we haven't prepared for. It's not *that* hot, perhaps about 78°F (25.5°C), so it's not as if we'll get heatstroke, but as we step out of the tent, the air folds over our heads like a warm, wet blanket. Sweat breaks on my brow even though I've done nothing more than pick up my backpack.

I'm hopeful, though. Maybe today is the day I'll get into the meditative quality of the hike. I'll think those big thoughts, perhaps have an epiphany or two. I don't even care what they're about. Writing? Teaching? Moving into the new house? Any realization will do, big or small.

We hike away from Anchorage and down the deserted beach. It's just us, headed toward a small orange triangle that flags the way. We wind our way past the granite Elephant Rock formation and cut through a small pass to the tidal inlet on the other side. This spot looked like a lake yesterday when we hiked down, but now that the tide is out, we'll cross it in our water shoes.

I'm hoping for no quicksand. None. Zero. Not even a little bit. As a Gen-Xer, I remember the reruns of the black and white *Tarzan* television show. They all seemed to deal with quicksand, and it was something that haunted my childhood nightmares. I forgot to google if Abel Tasman has quicksand, and of course, with no signal, I can't google now, so I step into the mud, then into the water while holding my breath. I use my poles as antennae, poking them in front of me. Because I've studied how to survive quicksand—of course I have—I walk ahead of Lala, just in case. Only one of us needs to fight this fight. If I go down, I'll stick a pole behind my hips and lean back, slowly moving my legs back and forth, letting water fill in around them until I'm floating, and then I can wriggle to the edge. Basically, I'm a goddamn hero for walking ahead of my precious spouse.

Behind me, Lala takes objectifying photos of my calves.

We make it across with absolutely no quicksand death at all (which makes the crossing very similar to the rest of my life). We find that faucet Merisha had mentioned, rinse our feet, and put on our hiking socks and boots. Then three bouncy young Brits pass us, but at least they're not centenarian Kiwis showing us up, so we allow the youth their springiness.

The high that comes with making it across the tidal inlet lasts as we walk past old off-grid beach houses only reachable by boat or kayak. The high lasts to the top of the first hill where we eat apples and glory in how quickly we've climbed to such a height.

Then the hike gets hard.

For me, at least. Lala is in high spirits, and I trail her, happy to let her lead now. I feel overheated and puny. Sweat is coming from pores I didn't know I had, and the breeze has died, which makes the mugginess even heavier.

I got a blister on my little toe yesterday. Today I've wrapped it in duct tape, usually a surefire blister reliever, better than moleskin or Band-Aids, but it's still plaguing me. It's so big that I'm just tromping on the blister with its next-door-neighbor toe with every step. I feel dizzy at times, but honestly, I'm pretty sure that's just anxiety over whether we have enough water.

The more I worry about water, the thirstier I get. I allow myself to drink, of course, but each time, I imagine us running out in hour six or seven. My clothes are as wet with sweat as if I'd fallen into the tidal streams we crossed. What happens when you run out of water in your body? When you have nothing left to sweat? I didn't google that either, but it can't be good.

Also not good: parts of the trail have washed out in landslides. All winter, we've watched hills in Wellington slip, sometimes closing roads for weeks or months. Out our front window at home, we've been watching them repair a "wee" slip for almost a year now, and they're still not done.

Here on the trail, slips happen, and then the hardiest of the hardy Kiwis go out and carve new paths above and through them (or hell, I don't know, it's probably a solo eighty-two-year-old woman named Jean with her gardening trowel).

I *hate* these newly repaired sections. I've never been great with heights. As I pick my way along some sections that can't be more than fourteen inches wide, I imagine myself tumbling to my death, letting the scene play out in front of my eyes. Lala, horrified, screams my name from above. But she mustn't climb down to me—she knows our only hope is for someone to come along to get help. Someone does, a young man with strong legs and the fervent desire to save a life, but it's a two-hour run for him back to Anchorage where, hopefully, someone can scramble a medical helicopter. Meanwhile, I've lost too much blood, and Lala goes home a widow to the mortgage she won't be able to pay without my income.

I think this through every single time I pick my way along these paths.

Lala is kind, encouraging me along. Believing in me. *You can do it. I'm right here.* I don't share the grisly images I see on the backs of my eyelids. She was a young widow when I met her, and even though I know I'm being ridiculous in my fears, I still don't want to put into her head the thought of losing her second wife.

Then I get my chance to repay her kindness.

Bees.

We've traded places, and I'm walking ahead of her when a bee flies in front of her face. As she is prone to do when a bee is in her immediate vicinity, she bolts. Without thought, she simply runs forward, into me. The path is narrow here, the slope falling steeply to our right, so I throw my arms out and dig my feet into the ground, refusing to let her push past me on either side.

I turn to face her. "It's gone."

She comes to, her eyes losing that spooked-colt look. "Sorry. God, I'm sorry."

This, I can help with.

I make her walk in front, so that the bees we disturb fly in front of me, not her.

We make a good team. We always have.

Then we reach the combo pack. It's the boss battle, two for the price of one.

There's been a slip, an enormous one. The path is crudely cut and ridiculously narrow. I can barely breathe as we make our way over the highest, thinnest section of fresh dirt that's mostly sand. Lala says soothing things and I pray to everything I believe in, and we make it over the steep part.

But then we see it: in the freshly disturbed dirt wall next to the path, there is a swarm of wasps. They fill the total width and distance of the path until it turns in a switchback. To move forward, we'll have to walk *through* the swarm.

Lala's face is a mask of fear.

"You can do it," I say.

"No." She shakes her head. "Impossible."

"I know you can."

"I won't."

"I'll go first." I walk slowly through the waist-level swarm. I'm not normally scared of bees or wasps, but I have to admit the low roar of their buzz is terrifying. When I get to the switchback, I find more bad news. Wasps are swarming the wall of that path too.

Lala sees it on my face. "There's more?"

I nod.

"I can't. I'm going back."

We've been walking for about four hours, but I bet she's fifty percent serious. Maybe more. "You can do this."

I've never seen her look this scared. "Can I just run—or fall—down the slip to where the path turns?"

I shake my head. If she does that, she'll land right on top of the second swarm. "You just have to do it." I've forgotten the pain in my foot and how thirsty and how anxious I've been. I only want one thing: for her to be okay. "I'm right here. Go slow."

"I have to go *slow*?"

I know, because I *have* googled this plenty, that if she gets stung within three meters of the hive, the pheromone the angry wasp emits will request backup from its friends. If she gets stung, she'll have to move slowly and smoothly past the hive—any flapping will aggravate the swarm, and the dark clothing she's wearing will make it worse. Other sources say to run quickly and smoothly for a hundred feet if you're stung—wasps won't usually fly so far to protect their nest. But if she runs forward that far, she'll go off the cliff and into the rocky water far below.

From somewhere deep inside, my 911 voice rises. I haven't used it in almost seven years, but it's strong and it knows exactly what to say. "You will *walk* through them now. You *will not run*."

"I can't." Her eyes beg me not to make her do this.

Dispatcher Rachael expands along with the voice. I am a mountain of calm, drawing her toward the safety of my body. "You will. You will do it *now*. Take a deep breath in through your nose. Now, hold your breath as you walk forward slowly."

Possibly confused by the new instructions, she walks forward, her eyes screwed almost all the way shut.

When she's halfway down, I say, "Now breathe out slowly through your nose. As slowly as you can, that's right. Keep moving. You're doing great. *Keep walking to me*."

Then she's through and we're past the wasps, and she's hugging me, and I'm kissing her.

"You were so brave," we tell each other. "You were so brave."

Then, of course, the next thing we have to do is keep walking.

By the time we reach Bark Bay, I'm exhausted from the adrenaline crash. Lala's panicking every time a bee flies in front of her, and this happens often. We try to eat our lunch, but bees and wasps are drawn to our sweat as well as the meat and sweet mustard in our sandwiches. Now that she's not near a nest or a cliff, she can run, and she does, eating standing up, darting away as bees buzz her meal. As she comes back from her most recent gallop, I hear her mutter, "I need a Valium." I can tell she's not kidding, and I'm shocked. In our relationship, I'm the one who's always chosen to handle stress using substances, not her.

The sign near our picnic table displays the distance to our end point. "Awaroa, 4.5 hours."

I can't do it.

I'm in pain. I'm exhausted.

I don't *want* to do it.

We call it. We're four hours in, and it's enough.

I trudge down to the beach to talk to a water taxi skipper who's just pulled up. He's going southbound, but he radios the next (and last) northbound boat of the day. There are two seats left, and he reserves them for us.

When it arrives an hour later, as we wade through the water and up the gangway, I feel a stab of guilt. We've done twelve kilometers in four hours. I simply don't have another four and a half hours in me, and my water is more than half gone.

That stab of guilt, though, is blown away by the cold wind and salt spray as we bounce our way to the lodge. I'm giddy to be cool for the first time all day. Giddy that soon I can drink all the water I want. Just thinking of it, I greedily stick the end of my hydration pack's hose in my mouth and suck the bag dry.

Our room at the lodge is luxurious but *filled* with mosquitoes. We shut the windows, and while Lala showers, I kill at least fifty of the little shits. We're traveling so light that I have nothing to use as a weapon except the René Magritte journal I bought at the Guggenheim in Venice. I'm *done* with bugs, so I use it. I hear Lala laugh in the bathroom every time she hears me smash a big one. I regret nothing.

I drink all the water I want.

Showered, in a mosquito-free room and covered in fresh bug spray, we nap.

It's perfect.

At dinner, we learn that most casual hikers do today's planned trek in two days. Not in one. (Okay, I'm sure the superfit octogenarian trampers do it in one day, but we aren't superfit, and we're babies, only in our fifties. We're still in training to be hardy elderly Kiwis.)

This knowledge elates me—we didn't fail! On the contrary, what geniuses we were to jump into that water taxi and skip over those kilometers!

I sip my ginger ale with relish, chasing it with yet more delectable water. "Those kilometers were probably just more of the bee park, anyway."

Lala scowls. "I hate the bee park."

"You were very brave."

She perks up. "I was!"

"Did you like my 911 voice? Firm but kind."

"Bossy."

"I was surprised I still had it in me."

"*I* wasn't surprised."

"Oh, come on. It was helpful, right? When I told you to hold your breath and exhale slowly?"

"Ha." She smirks at me. "I didn't do that."

I'm surprised. "My 911 voice didn't work on you?"

She relents a little. "I think it would work on anyone who didn't hear that bossy voice *all the time*."

"Unfair," I say. "That wasn't vanilla bossy. That was saving-your-life bossy."

Slowly, she lifts one eyebrow over her beer. Then her mouth quirks into a smile. "You *did* save my life. I was just going to run off the edge of the cliff."

"I'm glad you didn't."

When a bee flies through the dining room, she stays in her chair. She barely even squeaks.

. . .

The next day is a rest and relaxation day at the lodge. I finish the two books I've been reading and start a third. We both swim in the warm, clear-blue water. I give Lala a minor heart attack when I'm floating on my back looking at the sky and a water taxi comes straight at me, but I hear it in time and get out of the way. We eat pizza on a lawn, laughing at the cheeky weka (ground hens who look a bit like kiwi birds) that want to steal our pizza crusts. We feel so great we even consider taking a short day hike. Then we remember what the desk receptionist probably meant by "short day hike," and I get a massage while Lala reads.

The day after that, we lace up our boots again. If we make it through this almost-sixteen-kilometer hike, it will be our longest hike of the trip.

I'm determined to make it the entire way today.

And, importantly, the water taxi doesn't run this far north around Separation Point, so my determination is more like acceptance that we *must* make all the mileage today. We have no other option but to do so.

The day starts well, with sun and a cool breeze. We follow the trail through a meadow filled with summer flowers.

And then it *stays* good.

The hills are intense, yes. But we're gasping not only at the steepness, we're also gasping every time we round another corner to face yet another astonishing view. With our cameras, we try to capture the feeling of hiking through what feels like true jungle, only to see white sand, crystal blue water, and far in the distance, the edge of the North Island, where we live. (Where our new house is!) The pictures, though beautiful, can't capture the feeling. Even as we snap them, we know they can't catch the way our hearts race and our breath gets stuck at the top of our lungs at the ridiculous beauty.

The downhills are also intense, but they always let us out on yet another glorious beach that makes up part of the trail. Most Abel Tasman trampers don't go up and over the top, so we see almost no one. These beaches are ours.

At a heavenly beach ingloriously named Mutton Cove, we sit on a driftwood log in the shade of an enormous macrocarpa tree. I'm determined to get enough calories into us to forestall a crash later, so even though it's not lunchtime yet, we sit with our feet in the sand and shovel food into our faces.

Then we hear a splash.

There, at the end of the cove: a pod of dolphins, leaping and playing as if they've been waiting for us to appear. I run toward the water. I hoot and holler, knowing that dolphins actively like humans, and yes, I'm right, they come toward us.

We're stunned.

We're enchanted.

When I kiss Lala, I feel her smile under my lips. I taste apple and the salt of her sweat. My heart climbs into the sky with joy. This might be the most beautiful place I've ever been in my life.

We watch until they are gone.

After that, there are more hills, including the last hill that never seems to end. We climb that bastard for what feels like forever but is probably more like ninety minutes, convinced that around *this* next bend, we'll finally reach the top.

Still, I'm enjoying myself. We've left behind the bee

portion of the hike, for which Lala is very grateful. That said, I get a bumblebee the size of a small kitten caught in my braid for a while, and I'm shocked by the volume its rage can produce so close to my ear (I free it using my hat to grab it like the kitten it is, and we all bumble on our way).

And today?

Today is the day I finally get my epiphany.

It's not about our new house or how we'll decorate it.

It's not about any of the books I'm writing or want to write.

It's this: I've already found what I came looking for.

I'm already meditating.

As we hike the endless hill, I have no thoughts in my mind. Only: *step, place right pole, step, place left pole.* Gasp at the view. Gasp at the sheer stubbornness of this hill. *Step, place right pole.*

Oh, my god. I've been in the moment this whole time. The only time I haven't been in the moment is at night when I'm anxiously trying to plan the next day.

I haven't been meditating *on* anything.

I haven't been thinking *about* anything.

Thoughts, of course, have filtered through, and I chat off and on with Lala, but mostly, I've been thinking nothing at all. I've just been following the path, living inside my body at that very moment.

Feeling the blister grow.

Watching the dolphins.

Kissing Lala's salty mouth.

Swallowing delicious plastic-tasting water.

Stepping over tree roots.

Splashing through mud.

I've been right here.

. . .

The last day is the easiest, only three short hours. It's bittersweet. I've finally found my groove, and I could walk like this for the rest of my life. We make our way over another wee (huge) tidal flat and I'm not scared of quicksand even once. We get lost for a few minutes, and I almost regret that we so easily figure our way back to the path.

I don't want to stop.

But I also can't wait to get home so we can pack to start the next chapter of our life in Aotearoa.

We take our last few steps of the hike, and anticlimactically, eat our bananas and a bag of chips. Then we wait on the beach for our water taxi, which we'll take back to our starting point, where our car is waiting for us to drive it onto the ferry and take it home tomorrow.

The boat arrives. We splash through the waves and up the gangway. It's full, every seat taken. At the end of the forty-five-minute ride, the skipper heads full-tilt at a tractor that's idling in the surf, water up to the middle of its tall tires. We crash-land on the boat trailer invisibly attached to the tractor, and we scream with surprised laughter and joy. The skipper disembarks, wades through the water, and takes his place on the seat of the tractor. He pulls us onto the beach and we ride through town, the diesel smoke blowing into our faces.

I've been chatting with the man in front of us. He has a North American accent, and he's with his partner and their three children.

"So," he says over the roar of the tractor. "Where are you from?"

"Wellington," I say proudly. Firmly. "Originally from the San Francisco area. What about you all?"

His face lights up, but he doesn't immediately answer. I can almost see the wheels turning in his head as he rearranges the words he usually says.

Then, with a proud smile and a joyful voice, he says, "We're from Invercargill."

Lala and I haven't been there yet, the city at the very south of the South Island. I nod, waiting for him to fill in the rest.

"But we're originally from the Seattle area."

I don't have to ask him if they're staying.

I know the answer.

Chapter 16

Packing, Again

The first time we saw our house, a week before the hike, we knew.

When we pulled up in front, Lala breathed, "I want it."

Me too. But I wasn't brave enough to say it.

The house was a 1930s bungalow, painted light yellow with green trim. Set on a wide block lined with similar-vintage houses, it nestled in a sleepy Wellington village best known for its world-class bird sanctuary. When the realtor opened the door for us, he was apologetic about the brightly painted walls. He couldn't possibly have known that our old walls had been painted these exact colors of red, orange, and yellow.

We walked through, hearts pounding.

My dog-like nose sniffed. The air smelled dry. This was such a rarity in Wellington homes, especially empty ones, but I detected not one whiff of mildew or mold. Instead, I smelled the gleaming wood floors, which were original polished rimu planks that had been varnished to a sheen so glossy they looked wet.

It turned out that while the approved bank loan felt like an outrageous amount, it wouldn't get us much in a market that was a lot like the San Francisco Bay Area. Most of the places we'd looked at had big problems. *This one's very damp, this one's quite moldy, this one is actually wet and squishy, wait, where's the glass that should be in this window frame? Do you think that's load bearing? Is it* safe *to stand on this?* We viewed a house with a stunning harbor view that couldn't make up for the hundred steps down the hill to the front door. We both got vertigo the one and only time we went down. We looked at a place just two blocks from the beach, which felt too good to be true, and then we checked the flood and tsunami zones and learned that in just a couple of years, it would be uninsurable.

This house, though.

The realtor pointed to a register on the floor. "That," he explained proudly, "is where warm air comes up. It's called central gas heating."

We gasped. We'd never seen the like in any house we'd visited in New Zealand, not once. There'd been no central heat in any of the Airbnbs, in none of our friends' homes, and in none of the open houses we'd toured. In fact, the week before, a realtor at a different property had bragged, "This house has central heat." Then he'd pointed to a single plug-in wall heater in the center of the hallway.

In our house-to-be, I stuttered, "As in, there's a furnace? A gas furnace? Like, the heat is ducted? It comes up into all the rooms?"

He nodded and started to explain how it worked, but Lala interrupted him. "Oh, we *know* how central heat works!" Her eyes met mine, and my heart rang like wind chimes.

Despite the spitting drizzle outside, the house felt bright

and welcoming. In the backyard, a small sitting area looked up at a terraced hill covered with native plants. I climbed the hill and gazed on the rooftops of the village and a line of green hills draped with mist.

Lala emerged through the back door as I came down the steps from the hill. I could only look at her sideways, not daring to meet her eyes again. If I did, we'd inevitably betray our excitement to the realtor, and we couldn't do that.

He hovered nearby.

I touched an exterior windowsill. "Hmm, some rusting nails out here, huh?"

"Owners anxious to sell," he said. "If someone offered under asking, they might consider it."

"Hmm," I said again, attempting a frown, shoving down my cartwheeling heart.

In the car, Lala spun to face me, her expression alight. "Let's make an offer."

"Right now?" I loved it, but it was at the very top of our price range, and it would be a push, financially.

"It's *perfect*."

"It is, right?" There were only three steps to the front door and none to the back. There was a hill behind it, but it was set on the flat. It wasn't in a flood-prone area. Those things were astonishing, given Wellington and our budget. The property report looked okay, with some water damage to a few areas that needed fixing, but nothing that looked pressing. No issues with damp or mold, another Wellington miracle.

"You really want to make an offer?"

Her voice was firm. "Yes."

I texted the realtor, and ninety minutes later, our daringly lowball offer was accepted by the sellers.

. . .

We are giddy. We're thrilled.

Up until now, we've considered ourselves lucky to be able to afford to rent in this, our favorite city. To buy? We'd barely dared to dream, always thinking that someday we would have to break our own hearts and leave Wellington to buy a home somewhere else.

Excitedly, we tell our friends and family. "We bought a house!"

And an odd thing keeps happening.

Our friends and family are *shocked* by our house purchase, even though buying a home in New Zealand was always part of our long-term plan.

My dad says, "But...that means you're staying, I guess?"

Our pandemic podmate Megan says, "Well, *shit*. So you're really not going to buy back your old house and be my neighbor again."

My best friend says, "Wow. I suppose that means you're actually staying there."

Lala's dad says, "Well, if you're not coming back, I guess I'll have to get out your way at some point. It's a long flight, though. It's really long."

This shared reaction stumps me. What did they think? That we'd sold our house and most of our things, but we were just kidding? *Hey! We're back! Did you miss us?*

I reach out to movers.

The first moving company asks about the access to the premises. I'm truthful. *Fifty steps, some narrow, others uneven. The parking is difficult but I'll hold a spot with my car for the truck.*

The owner writes back, *Sorry, but my guys work really hard and I'm trying to spare them a bit.*

Well. My union-loving socialist roots adore this about New Zealand. I love that it shuts down for a month in summer over Christmas. Hospitals and grocery stores stay open, but most other businesses are closed. Even though the house sale is final on the fourteenth of December, we can't get the keys to our house until the twentieth of January because that's when banking officials and lawyers go back to work, and we need our solicitor to do all the magic moving of money. Even when I can't get my prescription refilled because Unichem (the CVS of New Zealand) is closed for the holidays, I love the country's commitment to workers' rights. So I do respect that the owner of the moving company is turning down cash on the barrelhead to take care of his guys.

But there's no way Lala and I can carry our furniture and boxes down those steps. We've gotten stronger and healthier living here, but hardy Kiwis we are not yet. That's a firm no-go.

I contact another moving company and when asked about access, I say, *A few stairs.* That owner, though, is no dummy. *I looked at your address on Google Street View, and I'm sorry that I must decline, I'm sparing my guys the difficult stuff.*

To the third company, I say, *A lot of stairs. We're desperate. Name your price.*

I never even hear back from that one.

So I can hardly believe it when the fourth company accepts. Will they show up? I've read accounts of local movers sending a text the night before they're supposed to arrive saying they can't come, and if that happens, the only option will be to pack our passports, a couple of changes of clothes, and walk away, leaving everything behind, taking with us only a fresh start and a vague regret for leaving all our money and thousands of diary pages behind.

Now the packing gets real.

We turn into monsters.

Is it the trauma of last time? It's almost exactly two years since we decided to leave the US, since we did one of the most exciting and difficult things we've ever done. Is that what's making us growl at each other every eleven seconds?

For my part, it feels like more than just grumpiness.

I feel *mean*, as if someone has replaced the normal bubbles in my blood with something more acidic. There's more bile than oxygen running through my veins. I want—need—to control everything around me. I need to be right. *So* right. Unfortunately for her, the only person to prove my bone-deep rightness to is Lala, who is packing all wrong.

Since she's still funemployed while I'm working full time, she's "supposed" to be packing the house while I work.

But she's not doing it the right way, nor is she doing it fast enough.

Oh-so-helpfully, I offer suggestions, and when Lala gets offended, I huff and puff her out of my way and redo what she's just done. *Look. You're holding the tape gun wrong. Do it this way.* While I'm at it, I snap when she doesn't wipe down the kitchen counters after she's done the dishes. Steam fills my soul when I see a beer can ring on the shitty melamine kitchen table. I grit my teeth when she walks too loudly. When she laughs at something funny on her phone. When she breathes.

Lala's no angel, of course. If I'm snapping at her, she's snarling back. But I'm meaner. I'm *trying* not to be—she has no idea how hard I'm trying. The criticisms I lob at her like perfume-bottle-sized Molotov cocktails are nothing compared to the North Island-sized volcanoes I've locked inside my chest.

I'm miserable. And I'm scared.

It feels like we're leaving our home country and moving to a new land—no, wait, we did that already. That adventure was worth it. We threw off our shackles, unsticking ourselves from the lives we'd been mired in. We launched out into the unknown, totally free.

Now, though—what are we *doing*?

Okay, I know exactly what we're doing. We're pouring every fucking dime we made from selling our California house into real estate that will tie us down again to one place. Far—so far—away from our families, we're taking on a mortgage with a high repayment each month, because we want to pay it off in fifteen years. We're sticking ourselves in place again. On the other side of the world.

I gasp awake at night and stare up into the darkness as Lala snores. I want to grab at her, to drag her awake. *We can run away. Let's just put the boxes into storage or throw them into the harbor, and we can get on a boat or a plane and go somewhere. Mexico. Vietnam. We can stay on the run.*

Tonight, Lala has made biryani for dinner. I'm grateful but only picking at it.

Lala says, "What if we're making a mistake?"

What if we're making a mistake? A sharp sheen of sweat covers my chest with hot prickles.

How *dare* she?

I'm the only one allowed to have that thought. She's supposed to be the bolsterer, the one who believes. After all, *she's* the one who, when we first saw it, said, *I want it.* She was the one who'd said, *Let's make an offer.*

If she had said, *Let's find something cheaper. This is great, but it's at the top of our price range, right? Let's keep looking,* I'd have been disappointed, but I would have nodded and gone along with her. I'd also desperately wanted two other houses that she had good reasons for not wanting, and I recovered just fine.

What if we *are* making a mistake? My chest thumps a staccato rhythm.

"We're not," I say.

Then I wait for her to agree with me.

She says nothing.

"Right?" I move the saltshaker to the side so I can grasp her hand. "We're not making a mistake."

She doesn't curl her fingers into mine.

I tighten my grip. "This has all gone perfectly. Just like everything else has." This entire adventure—everything has slipped just right, dominoes falling perfectly into place. Lala's visa, house sale, perfect apartment, bank approval for a mortgage, house closing two weeks before our lease is up.

Lala says, "Yeah. It's all worked out." But her voice is the one she uses when she's not engaging with me: flat, toneless.

I scooch forward in my chair and pull her hand closer to me. "Aren't you excited?"

"Sure." She doesn't meet my eyes.

The next words come even though I don't want them to. "Oh, come on, aren't you happy we're moving into a new house together? The two of us! New adventure!"

"Yeah."

A chill goes through me. "Do you even *want* to live with me there?"

"Would it matter if I didn't?" She shrugs. "It's too late now."

It's a tiny nuclear detonation, an explosion the size of the saltshaker. I drop her hand and scoot backward. "Wait. What?"

"It's *fine*, Rachael."

My jaw aches. "You don't want to do this?"

"I didn't say that."

"You're that unhappy with me?"

A sigh is all I get.

Lala has never, ever doubted our relationship. At least not within my hearing, anyway.

"I've been that awful?"

She finally meets my eyes. "You've...it's been hard."

I choke out, "But...is it going to be okay? It's going to be all right. Right?"

Her gaze slides away again. "It'll be fine."

The day we move, a cyclone roars into Aotearoa. The movers arrive dripping wet and they're not going to get drier as they go.

I realize, too late, when they're already tromping through the apartment, that the carpets, once white (well, whiteish-gray and stained in spots), will probably never recover. I should have thought of this—I should have bought drop cloths and covered the floors, but it's been summer and not raining, and now I'm too tired to panic over it. So we won't get our deposit back.

I'm just happy they're here. We've hired these men to move our boxes and furniture, yes. But each one of the fifty steps up to our apartment fills me with guilt, and I want to throw dollar bills at each of the movers as if they're pole dancing in Magic Mike outfits. That won't do, of course, as New Zealand believes in paying everyone a living wage and discourages tips of any kind. No dollar-bill throwing will be done.

But I do say, "Hey, on the unload side, you guys want pizza?"

All three nod. "Yeah, yeah. Pizza's good."

"What kind do you want?"

They shrug. "Whatever."

"Pepperoni? Meat? Veggie?"

They shrug again. "Anything's fine, yeah."

I'm desperate to please them, to make the steps less painful, to thank them for doing this job that Lala and I would rather die than do ourselves. "You like Hell Pizza?"

Hell is the fancy pizza, double or triple the price of Domino's. It's not the pizza that broke college kids buy. And it's exactly the right thing to say. They shoot delighted looks at each other and grin. "Hell? Really?"

Another says, "Hell, yeah!"

"Should I just choose some? Anything you don't eat?"

"Nah, yeah, anything's good." More joyous looks. "Hell! Nice!"

I spend a hundred and fifty dollars on pizza for them that day. They have more pizza than they can eat, even after trudging up and down stairs and into our new house for more than four hours. In the final packing moments, I find a bottle of champagne someone gave us, and I offer it to them too. I invite them to eat inside, but they politely refuse, standing in our driveway at the open door of their now-empty van, eating pizza and swigging from the bottle in rain that's slowed to a warmish drizzle.

When they leave, the pizza I bought for us has gone cold. The air fryer is packed, we still need to buy a microwave, and we're too tired to figure out how to use the mysterious oven.

But in this moment, nothing matters.

We sit on the floor of our new house and eat cold pizza over the small metal table that held plants in my old office.

Even with mud tracked in from the rain, our hardwood floors gleam. They shine.

"We're home," I say.

"My whole body hurts," Lala says.

I poke the pizza box. I bought too much for us too. "Oh, my god, we don't have a fridge." Our new one doesn't arrive for another two days.

"Doesn't matter."

"What, we're going to eat unrefrigerated pizza tomorrow?"

"Us and a million college kids. It'll be fine."

I gaze into the dining room, now full of boxes. "How do we *have* so much stuff?" We brought sixty-seven boxes to New Zealand, but we have more than a hundred. Way more.

"I kept wondering that too, but we bought all Sam and Cassidy's stuff, remember?"

A quick beat of relief. "Oh, yeah. I can't believe the movers carried all of those down the stairs. Mostly one box at a time."

"They asked me what we did, did you hear that?"

I shake my head and stuff another bite in my mouth, knowing while Lala will probably eat the pizza tomorrow, I'll be too neurotically worried about food poisoning. Might as well stuff my face now. Around a bite of chorizo, I say, "Why did they ask that?" New Zealanders never ask about occupations.

"The books. They'd never seen so many boxes of books."

I laugh. "I asked one of them if he thought we were hoarders. He said, 'not quite but maybe getting there.'"

"And we barely have anything. Like, most people in the States have soooo much more than we do."

"Because they have storage. Big closets." With a typical older Kiwi house, one drawback is the almost nonexistent closet space.

Lala says, "They liked the pizza."

"Thank god," I say. "They really liked the pizza."

We look around. My neck screams at me that it shouldn't be abused the way I've been abusing it. From here on the lounge floor, I can see into the glassed-in front porch with its lead lights. The stained-glass flower glows in the late-afternoon sun just peeking out from the clouds. I loved it the first time I saw it, but it hasn't hit me what kind of flower it is until this moment. "Oh, my god, Lala." I point. "It's an iris."

"No way." She looks. "It *is*."

My poor neck swivels as I look up at the ceiling, covered with original art nouveau embossed plaster. It's almost a hundred years old. All I've noticed till now is the intricate design, but not the detail.

I point up. "Irises."

Lala's jaw drops.

In Oakland, for fifteen years, we lived on Iris Street.

Iris was our home.

Now we're here, in the iris house.

My heart is full. My neck is killing me. The dining room is so full of boxes that I want to just throw them all out instead of unpacking them. We haven't killed each other. I still want to curl into Lala's body when we go to sleep tonight (as soon as I find the box I put the sheets in).

Something stabs me in the hip.

I dig the skeleton key out of my pocket and hold it up. "But this? Fucking ridiculous."

"It looks like the key to Fairyland in Oakland."

Fairyland was one of my favorite places in the world as a child. Other kids talked about Disneyland, but I'd never been there, and knew it couldn't be better than the legendary mini-adventure park in Oakland where storybooks came to life. Each child got a plastic skeleton key, a key to the kingdom of imagination.

The brass is heavy in my hand. "I love it. But I can't believe it's the only key to this house."

"We're getting it rekeyed."

"Immediately. Yes." I pause.

I'm not brave enough to ask what I think: *Will you feel stuck again?*

Instead, I say, "Do you...do you like me again?"

Her kiss is swift and sweet. "No. I love you again."

Chapter 17

Junebug

The exterior of the old Wellington Fever Hospital is a Queen Anne-style brick-and-timber building with multiple wings and long verandas, built for the previous pandemic more than a hundred years ago. It's rumored to be haunted, so as we walk down the hall, I keep an eagle eye out for spectral women flitting around corners or dog wraiths napping under any of the hallway benches.

But farther inside, the interior turns into the animal shelter it now is, no ghosts on display. Just concrete floors, thick metal doors, and a strong scent of industrial bleach.

My armpits sweat as we enter the dog pound area. Alice, a volunteer, shows us to an office with a couch covered by a chewed-up crocheted blanket. Then she goes to get Oakley.

I wait with shaking hands. We have *not* come here with the intention of leaving with a dog. We're only *meeting* dogs today. That's all.

The door flies open, and bang, there's Oakley.

Oakley is a *puppy*. She's gold and white, with tan eyes that look right into my soul. That is, they would look into my soul if she ever stopped moving. After a short cuddle, she leaps off our laps to gallivant up and down the walls, settling down to chew on the bookshelf.

Next to me, I can feel Lala's thoughts. *We're not ready for a puppy*. We dart a glance at each other and pull tiny grimaces, visible only in our eyes.

Lala grabs good cop and says, "What a sweetie she is!"

Shit, that leaves me with bad cop. "But she might be a little too much for us, honestly."

I feel bad—we kinda maybe sorta told the *smallest* itty-bitty lie to get into the shelter. In order to get in the doors, you must apply for a dog. When I called to ask about this practice, I was told, "That's just how it works. Once you're here, you can see any of the available animals, but you have to apply for one in particular." So we applied to see the dog who was on my screen at the time, and apparently it was Oakley. We didn't want a puppy, but the application got us entrance.

I try to smile winningly. "You know, we'd really like to see some adult dogs. Can we go look in the kennels?" That was how we found our darling Clementine, so many years ago. We went to look at a black dog and came home with the pit-bull-beagle creamsicle who'd been in the next cage over.

"I'm sorry, we don't allow that. We used to, but it's too upsetting to the dogs."

Huh. When Alice went to get Oakley, we heard the other dogs kick up a roar, presumably as she and Oakley walked past. But they're not constantly howling as they do in other shelters I've visited, so maybe they're onto something here.

"Okay, then, can you tell us about your other dogs? Oakley, sorry. No offense." Oakley gnaws on the concrete floor. No offense appears to be taken. "Here's what we're looking for. We want an adult dog, preferably older than two. Female. Any size, and any breed except lab because I'm allergic to them."

Alice gazes at us. I wouldn't want to play poker with this woman. She says, "I'm sorry, at the moment, pickings like that are slim."

"What about Monkee?" I've memorized the available adult female dogs on the website.

"I'm so sorry, she's unavailable right now."

"What about Kiki?"

"I'm so sorry, she's unavailable right now."

"Fig?"

"Unavailable. So sorry."

My face prickles with heat. "Do you have *any* adult females at all?"

"Adults are rare here, honestly."

I don't understand. Are those dogs on the website just plants to draw in suckers like us? Alice offers no other hints as to where the dogs might be. Are they being fostered? On trial to other families? Have they been euthanized? Or are Kiwis just more responsible about animal ownership?

"We have a lot of young dogs at the moment, since they're the most often surrendered."

Puppies are surrendered because puppies are the *worst.* Below us, Oakley whips out her Swiss army knife and starts dismantling the couch we're sitting on. She's *way* too smart a dog for us.

Then Alice says, "We do have another female, though. Same age, five months, a small staffie mix."

Staffie? Our hearts can't help but pitter-patter. We do love a bully breed.

Alice goes to get her.

Lala shakes her head. "A puppy, though?"

"We'll just look," I say. *I* don't want a puppy either.

I chant it in my head as the door opens. *I don't want a puppy. I don't want a puppy.*

The puppy who enters the room is small and chocolate-colored, with enormous light brown eyes. She has worried wrinkles on her forehead, but when she sees us on the couch, they smooth and she beelines for us. She leaps onto the couch and into our laps, curling her head down and pushing it against us, turning herself into an upside-down bagel as her tail whaps exuberantly. She stinks like urine and her fur is sticky with something I don't want to know about, but my arms are already hugging her. I wore my gardening overalls for a reason, after all.

Don't look at Lala.

I look at Lala.

Oh, no. We're sunk. Neither of us will admit it yet, but both of us know it.

"Can we take her for a walk?"

Alice says yes, and I try to ignore her knowing smirk.

We walk the little dog up a hill and down again. She doesn't pull but is eager to see and smell everything. She's a *baby*. A baby of a dog, and I can't stop staring at her.

"That's definitely pit bull," I say, hopefully. "Look at those forehead wrinkles." She gets them every time she hears a strange noise, but they smooth quickly and easily.

"Those ears, yeah. Pittie or staffie."

"But also definitely lab, right?" The only dog in the world I'm allergic to.

Lala nods. "Undeniably lab."

We sit on a bench, and the puppy jumps up onto our laps.

"Okay," I say. "Here goes." I rub my arms against the puppy's stinky fur. I let her lick my face and push my cheek against hers. I try to coat myself with her grossness, then I hold out my arms to watch for hives.

Nothing rises. I don't itch. Not a single bump comes up. "Maybe...maybe it's like with kittens, how I'm not allergic to them when they're tiny and then my body gets used to them as they get older?"

The hope in Lala's eyes could float a sunken galleon.

We ask for a seven-day trial, just in case this is a terrible idea, just in case I turn into one big walking, talking hive later, but we both know that if that doesn't happen, she's ours. Forever.

With the puppy firmly leashed in the back seat next to Lala, I chauffeur them from the pound to the pet store, where we buy a crate.

Here's the thing we don't understand, the thing no one has been able to explain to us in any book, forum, or YouTube video: *How* are you supposed to train a puppy to sleep in a crate all night when you first get them, if, during crate training, the point is to leave them inside it for a few seconds, then a minute, then five minutes, building up more and more time in the crate over the course of weeks? How do you gently build up training without forcing them to be in the crate, but at the same time force them to be in the crate all night from the very first night?

We go home, and Lala sets up the crate while I clean the back seat of the car where the puppy has (of course) peed.

The crate, we know, is a good idea. We have discussed—like the adults we are—what excellent dog parents we are going to be. We want her to be happy, to have a den of her own. We also want to be able to leave the house together someday. My old girl Clara was a perfectly crate-trained dog. But Clementine and Miss Idaho never accepted a single second of being in a crate (and oh, how we tried). I learned from them that I love to have a dog snoring in the bed. So does Lala. We literally bought a king-sized bed when we moved into our new house so that someday a dog would be able to sleep with us.

I'm done cleaning the pee out of the back seat, and I've finished skimming the entire internet, looking for and failing to find the how-to-crate-train-a-puppy-in-one-night answer.

In the living room, Lala has assembled the crate.

"Hey, here's a thought," I venture.

"Uh-oh."

"We're eventually going to give up and let her sleep on the bed with us. Right?"

She looks sheepish. "Probably."

"So why bother trying to get her to sleep in it at night at all?"

Her eyebrows draw together. "We crate-train-fail her right now? We just bought this thing."

"*Naps* in the crate, yes. But nights in the bed, with us."

Lala's face is pure relief. "So we do crate-train her. But not for night sleeping. That's cuddle time."

I lean down to scritch the dog's still-smelly-from-the-shelter head. "Exactly. Let's get her in the bath."

So.

This is it. This is the last step I've allowed myself to imagine for the last two years.

Leave the United States.

Find a city to love.

Rent an apartment.

Make friends.

Buy a home.

Adopt a pet.

We've done all the things. We've unpacked and had our first houseguest. We threw a housewarming party last month, and twenty-five people came, people I already love, people we didn't know before we came to this country. Our house feels like a home, and I'm so grateful that I get to do my beloved job from my sunporch office.

But before I step onto the existential rollercoaster of deciding what to do next, this particular chocolate-colored, wiggly-bodied, waggly-tailed, dream-come-true still needs a name.

We go through perhaps a hundred potential names in the first day. With no exaggeration, by day three, we're up to a couple of hundred ideas. Dolly, Maybelle, and Miss Kitty are strong contenders. But in the end, it comes to me on a walk. "Junebug?"

"*Ohhhh,*" says Lala.

"Right?"

It's Lala who completes the name, though, as we're resting on the back porch while Junebug chases a piece of cardboard.

"Professor Junebug," Lala says.

"*Ohhhh,*" I say.

"Right?"

After six weeks, the Professor is comfortable in her crate during naps. While I write, she likes to rest under my desk and chew on a sweet potato rawhide that the vet says is fine for her (I'm a nervous puppy mama, apparently).

Here are some things we've learned about our dog in six weeks.

Junebug is a bug. She is a cuddle bug and a snore bug. She's sometimes a silly bug, and *always* a love bug.

The Professor snorgles, which is a fancy-pants way of saying she likes to press her face into something (a thigh, a ribcage), then snore against it, like she's wearing a snorkel mask.

We've bought her so many toys, but the best toy she's had in her young life was the twelve-pack of toilet paper she shredded in the living room when I was out of town and Lala was preoccupied by eating the hottest Indian food she's had in years. Yes, that night, everyone was living their best lives.

She's reactive, a frustrated greeter. When she sees another dog, she wants to play with it *immediately*, and having never had rules around these things, she sees no earthly reason she shouldn't be allowed to. She rears up and pulls on her lead and barks and whines and jumps at the other dog, which goes the way you think it would.

We've been to one single day of a puppy training course where Junebug lost all her cool, barking at the other fifteen dogs in the gym. The trainer scared her to get her to stop barking, shaking a loud rattle at her. "You have to *show* her who's boss, see?" We fled at the end of the session, and I refused to go back.

Instead, we train Junebug three or four times a day, five to fifteen minutes at a time, and we've hired a private trainer. We're working on engage/disengage when we go on walks. The Professor knows sit, down, stay, touch, and drop it. She knows to gnaw her Kong toys on her mat, and she waits politely before entering and leaving the house.

A reactive dog isn't easy. But I want a happy, confident dog, and I'm willing to put in the work.

Lately we've been learning a calm settle. To work on it, I go into the backyard. I bring with me a book, the dog, and my natural stubbornness, which is almost a match for hers.

I leash Junebug close so she can't reach anything (she's already discovered the enjoyment of chewing on outdoor furniture). In an old running bag strapped around my waist, I have a massive amount of her kibble mixed with a few smelly treats for interest. The plan is to rain these treats down on her as soon as she relaxes.

That's it—that's the whole trick. I'm trying to teach her to lie down and rest.

The Professor is jumpy. She pulls on the leash, twists to look at me, then pulls the other way. Somehow she gets all four legs tangled in the leash, which shouldn't even be physically possible. *This* puppy, lying down and resting? Now? No way.

But eventually, she gets bored enough that she lies down. When her head hits the pavement, I count to ten, then I lean forward and place a handful of treats in front of her face.

She's so stunned that she doesn't even eat them at first. She pops up, giving me the sit she thinks I must want. I try to ignore her and look back at my book. I haven't turned a single page yet, too busy watching her in my peripheral vision.

Finally, she gobbles the kibble. Her body stays taut, a spring ready to sproing.

But then it happens again. She gets bored. She relaxes. Her chin lowers to the concrete, and her eyelids get heavy.

And again I play god, raining treats down on her from heaven. She's still startled but doesn't pop up as fast. After a while, it starts to work—she's getting it. She doesn't have to do anything. In fact, if she sees the treats coming and moves, my hand pulls back. In real time, she's learning that staying relaxed and floppy in the sun earns her the thing she wants.

So we sit there, working on this, our new favorite trick. I alternate dropping kibble between her paws and reading my book. I'm mostly shaded, but my feet rest in the same puddle of sun she lies in, and my body melts. My own eyelids are getting heavy.

It's then that I realize *I've* been tricked by learning the trick.

The calm settle? I'm teaching it to myself.

What if we could both learn things without struggling so much?

When Lala and I got hitched, we couldn't legally marry in the States, so we crossed the northern border. We paid Canada a hundred dollars, and a justice of the peace declared us legally married. The next morning, waking up in the hotel bed with Lala, I felt like she'd somehow gone from being my girlfriend to something more than a wife. She'd become my family. That simple piece of paper *shouldn't* have mattered so much, I know that. But it did. And when we were back home, the feeling didn't go away. Surrounded by our blended menagerie, her two dogs and my two cats, I felt at the center of a family we were building together.

We knew we couldn't have pets when we moved to New Zealand. Since the vast majority of rental units don't allow pets, until we could buy our own home, we'd have to do without.

I worried about empty nest syndrome—what would

Lala and I possibly talk about with no animals at our feet? Lala thought this worry was ridiculous, and thank god, she was right. We've spent the last two years talking—just the two of us. I still want to tell her all the things I want to tell another human being, and she apparently still wants to talk to me too.

Until I start to nod off, that is.

Embarrassingly, I usually toddle toward bed around eight p.m. I have a hard time going to sleep and I like to get up early, so going to bed when kids are still playing on the street is the only way I have a fair shot at getting seven hours of sleep.

But the first night Junebug was with us, I stayed up late and Lala went to bed early, so we could all bunk down at the same time. That night, we opened the door to the bedroom, and the freshly bathed puppy *leaped* into the bed and snuggled down under the blanket as if she'd slept in a people-bed every night of her life. Based on her age and the way her spay scar had completely healed, we believed she was surrendered to the shelter as soon as she was weaned, so this was probably not true. This was probably her first night in a bed. She was just born for French linen sheets.

And she did great. Junebug contentedly snorgeled her way through that first night.

So ever since, knowing that the puppy is a great sleeper, I feel free to go to bed at my normal toddler time.

Tonight, I putter around for a while, brushing my teeth and washing my face. I've added taking Junebug outside to my routine, and I stand for a moment on the hill behind the house, watching the lights of neighboring houses flicker through the trees.

I search the stars above, and there he is, Orion, still

goofing around up there in his eternal handstand. That's his natural position now, simply the way he looks.

The cosmos isn't upside down anymore.

This night sky is mine.

Junebug leaps into the air, trying to catch a moth, and my heart floats up and out of my chest. I am part moth, part dog, part somersaulting heavenly archer.

Then we go inside. I take Junebug into the living room, where Lala's watching a YouTube video about a Japanese video game. The Professor jumps up onto the couch and bagels against Lala's thigh. I kiss my wife goodnight. I pet Junebug's head.

And when I shut the living room door, I don't leave a "her" behind on the couch, as I did before Junebug. I leave a "them" behind me.

I wasn't feeling lonely before, exactly. But in this moment, somehow, I realize I feel like part of a pack. And oh, how I missed that feeling. I go to bed, knowing Lala and Junebug will join me soon, snoring our way to tomorrow, together.

Yes, you can argue that I'm stuck again.

I'm firmly entrenched in this life. There's nothing nomadic about anything I do. I have a mortgage and a dog. I have furniture, cooking pans, appliances. I have a washer and a dryer. I have a yard, and a garden, and neighbors, and friends. All these things require work and maintenance. They require attention and intention. But I want to give these elements my energy. I *choose* them.

And this is also true: I can unstick myself when I need or want to.

Could we move around the world again? Yes. (Do we want to? Jesus, *no*. But we could.)

Megan, our California neighbor whose golden ticket

comment prompted this whole move in the first place, recently came to stay for ten days. In the mornings, we'd both journal, me at my desk, her sitting up on the hill in her Baby Yoda PJs as the sun rose. She was right about what she told us way back then—she does clean up well. While she was visiting, I got used to seeing her in real clothes and makeup, but I have to say, I love her most in her pajamas, the ones I knew so well in the lockdown.

She trundled home, but my little sister Bethany is casting off her old life in the States soon. She'll be here to stay in just a few months. I can't wait to introduce her to my friends, to show her the streets I love, to introduce her to our dog. Maybe someday we'll get our other sister here. And maybe we won't. Proximity to the ones we love is a joy, but I've learned that it's also not required.

It turns out that the bands that hold the universe together can tolerate being turned upside down and right side up, can take being tumbled about until there's no more notion of up or down or left or right. Until all that's left is just what is.

This luxurious piece of knowledge allows me to relax into the moment in front of me.

I practice my calm settle. Here.

Right here, not where I'm stuck, but where I belong.

Epilogue

All is well in Wellington.

We've had our perfect, anxious Junebug for an entire year now, and while she's still frightened of things like oven sounds and unexpected fire hydrants, she's turning into a scent-work pro, acing her intermediate classes. And wonderfully, my sister Bethany has moved to New Zealand! Her caravan sits in our driveway, and Junebug has firmly adopted her as favorite auntie. I'm writing and swimming and playing badminton (a surprising turn of events) and teaching.

My writing students have recently sent me the *most* unexpected gift: a gift certificate to my favorite bakery, which means I can buy all the fruit bread I want. They *also* gave me a full sourdough kit, which comes with a goopy starter and three bags of flour stone-ground right here in Wellington.

My first reaction: *Oh, yay, I get to try making sourdough!*

My second reaction: *Oh, no, I have to learn the right way to make sourdough!*

I have always missed the bread train, no matter when it's rumbled down the gluten tracks. In my twenties when my friends passed around "Amish friendship starters," I politely held up my knitting and said *No, thanks*. In 2006, when the NYT no-knead was the rage, I no-kneaded a single loaf, which was delicious but not quite worth the lack of effort. In 2020, when lockdown Instagram filled with people's beautiful loaves, I continued to buy San Luis Sourdough off the grocery store shelves. Why work so hard for something that's so cheap?

But my attitude has to change now that I am a mother to a mother. "Mum" is written in Sharpie on the plastic tub of starter, which gives me a small shiver of maternal nerves. The instruction sheet, which somehow seems both over- and underwritten, leaves me with more questions than answers. It does say that if I'm not ready to start baking yet, I can pop Mum in the fridge for a while, thank god.

The starter safely resting in the chilly darkness, I start to read, diving into my studies like the eager freshman I am. I read *Flour Water Salt Yeast*, by Ken Forkish. Then I read *The Perfect Loaf*, by Maurizio Leo. I read *Sourdough*, a novel by Robin Sloan. Hilariously, I think at first that this is a memoir, and it isn't until the sourdough starter starts literally singing that I think *Huh?*

I join the sourdough subreddit and one migrainey day, during which I have to stay perfectly motionless but can still look at a screen, I spend nine full hours toggling between recipes and instructional videos.

Obviously, I can't start making bread until I find the perfect recipe.

It turns out there are a *lot* of sourdough recipes out there.

I watch every video I can find on keeping a well-fed vs. a starving sourdough starter. I study how to preshape the round boules, never having touched sourdough dough. I order a lame (a razor on a stick) to score the bread, and then I buy a new bread knife, knowing in my soul that our ancient knife is too dull. I save dozens of recipes, each time deciding that *this* is the one I'll try the next day, only to go on a new search before taking the plunge. This one is better. No, *this* must be the right recipe.

In the sourdough forum, people often say, "The only way to learn how to make sourdough is to make it." My toes curl in frustration. I want to learn the thing and then do the thing beautifully. I love it when people blurt, "That's your first time? I can't believe it! You're a natural!" Only then, having aced external observation, do I know I've studied enough.

But I worry about Mum, who's chilling in the fridge. I know I need to feed the starter, but what if I murder it by accident? Over on Reddit, people are always putting their twenty-year-old starters in a slightly warm oven to grow, only to have a family member turn it up to full heat, killing the starter dead. Each time this happens, the Reddit community mourns the member's staggering loss. I do take comfort in the knowledge that if I bork my starter, I can just drive across town and buy some more. Right? It isn't like mine is artisanal, made from the wild yeast I'd collected from the air in my kitchen and kept alive for decades. But still.

One morning, I wake feeling more confident than normal, so I pull Mum out, clad in her see-through plastic container. I feed the starter equal parts water and a careful blend of whole wheat and rye flour.

But oh, god, now where will I keep it? It needs to be

kept warm. The top of the refrigerator, a popular choice for many bakers, is chilly. Our oven has no light. Specially made proofing boxes are expensive, and while I could DIY one, I'm ready for action *now*, and therefore, impatient.

I go into the living room to check the temperature of the cabinet where our modem and router sit, another weird but popular proofing area.

Lala's playing a video game. I try to stay out of the way of the TV, but I have to block it for a moment. "Sorry, just a sec," I say, holding my hands up to the router as if it's a fireplace on a frosty night.

"What are you doing?"

"Can't find a warm enough place to put the sourdough starter."

"The top of the modem? That can't be a good idea."

I grimace. "Got a better one?"

"It *is* cold in here," she says in a sad voice.

I had promised Lala she wouldn't be cold. But our furnace recently died in a spectacular manner that stopped just short of killing us in our sleep. Good news: it'll be repaired in about a month. Bad news: a cold snap is moving through New Zealand, and when we wake, it's often 46 F (8 C) in the house.

I study her form on the couch. Handknit sweater, check. Blanket, check. Small space heater cranking out meager warmth, check. I can do better, though. "I'll make you a hottie."

While I'm rooting around in the linen closet, hunting for a hot water bottle, I hear her mutter, "*You're* a hottie." Then she shoots something on screen and whoops in triumph.

And as I fill the bottle with boiling water, I give my own small whoop as I'm struck by a flash of brilliance. Before I act on it, though, I tuck an extra blanket around Lala and slip the hottie underneath. She gives me a kiss in return.

Then, it's time for some hot sourdough action. I place another boiling-water-filled hottie in the microwave, pushed up against its back wall. I settle my freshly fed starter in front of it and close the door.

Anxiously, I check it every few hours, refreshing the hottie when it cools.

And huzzah, it *works*! The starter doubles, bubbling up and emitting a sweet banana scent.

Gathering my courage from this success, I embark upon making my first loaf. I follow my oh-so-carefully chosen recipe, which says to use 563 grams of water. The scale reads 564. Will that matter? Nerves flutter in my stomach. I use an eyedropper to lift out a dribble until it's exactly right. (Grams are so small! I honestly had no idea.)

Moving cautiously, I follow every instruction to the letter. The next day, after a nail-biting bulk ferment and a more relaxing overnight refrigerator nap, the bread comes out of the oven looking amazing and smelling even better. The exterior is a deep caramel brown, satisfying to tap. It has ripped a bit, my scoring not deep enough, and it's a little gummy in the middle. But I think it's the most delicious thing I've ever tasted.

Drunk on early bread success, I dive even deeper into the internet and into the literature. My first attempt was good, but I can do better. A few weeks later, I can do baker's math in my head, and I've made five more loaves, much to the delight of Lala and my sister Bethany. My impatience to get a "perfect" loaf is their gain.

"A little underproofed," I muse as they smear butter on freshly cut pieces.

"Better try again." Lala winks.

As I feed them the next loaf, I say, "This time I think it's overproofed. Look at that big hole."

"A fabulous place for Vegemite," says Bethany. "But yeah, you should keep trying."

"I'm so close to getting it right." I take a bite. "Oh, my god, I'm *so* close."

A few weeks later, when I next look up from the sourdough subreddit and blink like a flour-encrusted mole coming up out of its hole, the truth about sourdough drops into my brain like a shaft of golden light falling on a wheat stalk. I'm surprised it took me so long to figure out, and at the same time, it's completely unsurprising. It always takes me way too long to learn this kind of thing.

My divine revelation: Every recipe is saying the *same damn thing*.

In sourdough, you mix your three ingredients: flour, water, and salt (and starter, which is just flour and water that's formed its own leavening). You manipulate them to create gluten development. You let the dough ferment. Then you bake it.

The realization washes through me. I've been spending every free moment searching for the perfect recipe, but *there isn't one*. There's not even a perfect formula that works well for everyone. There are too many variables that prevent the One True Answer—my kitchen differs from your kitchen in heat and humidity. My oven doesn't work like yours. You'll never combine your flours in the same way I combine mine, and our protein levels will be wildly different.

There's just a general system.

A story, if you like.

There's a beginning (mix), a middle (ferment), and an end (bake). There's even an epilogue: eat and enjoy.

The way I arrive at my own perfect loaf will always differ from how anyone else gets to theirs. And yes, it's annoying but true—the more loaves I bake, the more I understand about the dough. Its jiggle tells me it wants more or less fermentation time. The way it springs in the oven tells me it wants more or less time at a higher or lower temperature.

I can let go of this tight feeling, the worry that I'm doing it wrong.

I'm doing it, and that's all that matters.

My mother said that when I was learning to speak, I'd trundle myself off to sit in a corner with my back to the room. I'd whisper the words I wanted to say over and over until I got the sound of them right. Only then would I turn around and speak them into the air, only after I'd proved to myself I knew what to say and how to say it well.

In my professional life, I spent ten years *not* writing as I searched for the best way to write. Each writing book and every professor seemed to teach a different method with a new set of rules. Of course, I couldn't decide to follow any rules until I knew them all, so I wasted years learning and thinking instead of, you know, actually writing.

I had thought everyone was saying different things about writing, and that it was up to me to sort out what was the best, the truest, the most helpful.

I failed to see the obvious. *Everyone was saying the same thing.*

Every piece of writing advice boiled down to this: your book should take your reader on a satisfying emotional journey by escorting them through a beginning, a middle, and an end. Oh, and by the way, it's just hard to write—you're not doing it wrong if you're struggling. Boom. That's it.

All the other stuff? The discourse about percentages and inciting incidents and pinch points and allies and turning points?

It was bonus info. Sure, those things could improve your books, but they were extra.

Sure, you *can* add jalapeño and cheddar cheese to your sourdough, but if your bread won't rise, you'll have to dump that gloppy mess straight into the compost.

When I realized I felt stuck in California, I started a quest for knowledge. With ever-increasing levels of franticness, I consumed memoir after self-help book about how people had made great and sweeping change in their lives—I wanted to follow their examples, not make up my own methods, which surely wouldn't be as good. When we decided to move to New Zealand, I researched and I optimized. I fretted and I worried. When we arrived here, I tried so hard to get the great search for home just right.

The correct answer, I've always felt, is out there. If I lift every single rock on the beach to peek underneath, I'll find it eventually, right? When I *do* uncover it, I won't have to worry anymore. Anxiety will drift away as I do the thing correctly. Perhaps even perfectly.

But I have to say, having the realization that *there is no right answer* smash into your consciousness is a lot better than heaving boulders out of the way to search for something that doesn't exist.

What if we'd trusted our guts and just moved straight to

Wellington, instead of circling it, instead of being scared that it wouldn't be the right home? Of course, if we'd done that, we wouldn't have gotten that first apartment with its incredible view of the harbor. We probably would have met different friends, we might not live in this house, maybe we wouldn't have Junebug (gasp).

What if that wasn't the right question either?

What if there were no questions?

What if there is just now? This moment. The moment in which I type these words, the one in which you hold this book. What if this moment is enough?

I stop looking for the best schedule for baking sourdough.

Instead, I mix water and flour when I feel like mixing them. My starter is named Lyle Loafett, and its yeast eats the flour, producing CO_2 bubbles that puff up my dough, making it delicious when baked. I have billions of little beastie pets, and I like making them happy. I do my own baker's math and make a bigger loaf for a dinner party. I mention to no one that it's a little underproofed. The loaf disappears in minutes so I don't believe they're sitting around wishing for an airier texture.

I've gone beyond obsessing over theory, and now I'm simply in love with being able to *make a loaf of bread*.

Honestly, I don't mind my predictability. While learning something new, I will stress out as I ingest every piece of available information in my quest to get it right. Then I'll realize there's no one best way and I'll enjoy just doing the thing in the way I want to. Every single time, I will forget this, an inevitable amnesia. If Lala had taken me by the shoulders, looked deeply into my eyes, and proclaimed, "There's no one right way to make sourdough," I would have agreed intellectually, but my process would have been the same.

Now, I take a breath. I eat the last slice of the most recent imperfect loaf.

In this memoir, I've written my story. It went like this: Feel stuck, abandon home, find a new life.

But I could have also written it like this: Love a person, take an adventure together, settle down (again) with her.

Or: Try to get things right, try so hard it hurts, remember for the thousandth time there is no right.

I like to reduce ideas to their simplest forms (flour, water, salt; beginnings, middles, ends), so here's the simplest form of this story: *Live a life.*

Or perhaps just: *Live.*

There's no best way to do this. Best doesn't exist. I'm not doing it wrong if I want to ignore the weeds in the yard and sit on the couch cross-stitching while listening to a Jodi Picoult audiobook. If I want to make three more loaves of bread this week, fabulous. It's also fine if I make none and instead buy a loaf of fruit bread from Shelly Bay Bakery at the waterfront market where Nella sees me coming and has my loaf bagged by the time I reach the top of the line.

I choose *this* life, which is a changeable system, not a fixed formula. More baths this week, fewer hikes. Next week? Perhaps I'll choose more writing, an extra swim, and coffee time with friends.

It's funny: I'm always trying to help my writing students understand at a deep, visceral level that there's no *right* way to write a book—there's just *their* way. But by sending me a living sourdough starter, they taught me that all over again. What luck I have. What love.

In the kitchen, I cut into the newest loaf, immediately calling for Lala and Bethany to come and witness my best open crumb so far. I slice them each a piece and we eat standing up, our eyes closing in rapture. Junebug gives an excellent sit, so she gets a bit too. The dough is sour from the lactic acid and tastes exactly like joy.

This, I must admit, I have done just right.

The End

About the Author

If you liked this book, please join Rachael's mailing list here, and get a FREE BONUS CHAPTER about the surprise wisteria vine she found in her Wellington garden, and why it was so important. Go here to join: RachaelHerron.com/wisteria

Rachael Herron is the internationally bestselling author of more than two dozen books, including thrillers (under R.H. Herron), mainstream fiction, romance, memoir, and nonfiction about writing. She received her MFA in writing from Mills College, Oakland, and she's taught writing extension workshops at both UC Berkeley and Stanford. She lives in Wellington, New Zealand with her banjo-playing wife and brick-eating dog.

Acknowledgments

My thanks, first and foremost, to my patrons at Patreon. Writing these essays for you as my life was coming apart and fitting back together was both my anchor and my privilege. Thank you for supporting me so beautifully. (Those who supported at that level are listed on the next page! Thank you!)

And to the Kickstarter backers—you blew me away. I still can't believe it.Your name might not be listed on the next page like the Patrons are, but your name is listed in my heart! Thank you, SO much.

Thanks also go to Monna McDiarmid and Damien Pitter, for showing us how to move around the world with your favorite person. Thanks to Emma Bannenberg, who taught me there are no wrong turns in Italy. Thanks to Catriona Turner, fellow around-the-globe mover, editor extraordinaire, and friend. And to Gillian Rodgerson, thanks for your impeccable eye!

My love and appreciation to the friends I left behind. You're always with me. Please come use the pull-out couch. Megan, come back. I mean it. That same (but different!) love and appreciation to my new friends, including (in alphabetical order because I can't rank you) Ali, Anne, April and Jules, Daniel and Aurora, Jenny, Jo, Leticia and Olivia, Melissa, Moira, Roisin, and Shelly. Thanks for catching me.

For my sisters, Christy and Bethany, always and forever.

And for Lala (again), thanks for letting me write about you. You make good copy, great coffee, hilarious jokes, and my world keep spinning.

Patrons

My thanks, always, to past, present, and future patrons at Patreon , including these who supported me during the time I was writing (and living) this book. Alphabetical by first name:

Afton Koontz, Aimee Threet, AK Mulford, Alex Woolfson, Alice Law, Alison Heath, Amanda Gibson, Amanda Taylor-chaisson, Amanda Ward, Amber Reed, Amy Draper, Amy Marchand Collins, Amy Norris, Amy Singer, Amy Teegan, Ana Strucelj, Andee Mazzei, Andreea Boboc, Angie Green, Anita Holmes, Anna Pohl, Annastasia Gallaher, Anne Wilson, Anne-Maree Gray, Anni Marjoram, Antonette , April Smith, Barbara Becc, Barbara Samuel O'Neal, Beate Wiechmann, Becky Allen, Beth Brown-Reinsel, Beth Wallace, Beverly Army Williams, Bonnie Craig, Brooke Sinnes, Bryan Souders, Caitlyn Britel, Cami Ostman, Camilla Lombard, Candace Floyd, Cara Finnegan, Cari Luna, Caro Dean, Carol Gunby, Caroline Gaudy, Carolyn Strug, Carrie Bishop, Carrie Sundra,

Cassandra Leach, Cassidy Thompson, Cassie Newell, Cat Fithian , Catherine Kittrell, Cathie Jones, Cathy Selmi, Catriona Turner, Caysie , Charlotte Dixon, Charlotte G., Cheri Merz, Cherry Hood, Cherryll Sevy, Chris Knowlton, Christabel Choi, Christine Halverson, Christine Nordell, Christy Brown, Cindy Hahn, Claire Chandler, Claire H. , Clare Lydon, Clarence Cromwell, Clark Huggins, Corrie Whitmore, Crys Cain, Crysta Parkinson, Cynthia W. Gentry, Dahlia Hamza Constantine, Dan Herron, Dana Strotheide, Darren Blake, Deb Sinness, Deborah Gudger, Diana ben-Aaron, Diane Huffman, Diane Lewis, Dominic Lim, Donna Ryan, Dorie, Doug Schneider, Edward Giordano, Eleanor Kos, Elizabeth Dunphy, Ellen Firinn Sanning, Ellen McCoy Baty, Ellie Ashe, Emberly Nesbitt, Emily Judds-Winograd, Erica Hughes, Erica K, Erika Barcott, Erin Hayes, Faye Whyte, Furious-teapot , Genevieve , Gladys Strickland, Grace Jeschke, Heather Bogart, Heather Golder, Heather Patel, Helen Conway, Helen Cosgrove-Davies, Holly Bowen, Holly Storck, Isabel Canas, J. Thorn, Jackie Faron, Jamie Miles, Jana Deck, Jana M Floyd, Janelle Hardacre, Janet Kornegay, Janine Bajus, Jason Poole, Jeanette LeBlanc, Jeff & Will, Jeff Elkins, Jen Cranston, Jenn Dellow, Jenni Clarke, Jenni Momsen, Jennifer Eisenberger, Jennifer Flunker, Jennifer Lauer, Jennifer Outland, Jennifer Sciubba, Jenny Andersen, Jenny Darlington , Jenny Grant, Jesse C., Jessi S. , Jessica Green, Jessica Honsinger, Jessica Mehring, Jill, Jill Ross Nadler, Jillian Price, Jjennifer Zeitler, Jo VanEvery, Joan Harris, Joanna Penn, Jodi Terry, Jody Julkowski Nelson, Johanna Spiers, Josee Smith, Juanami L Spencer, Jude Pilote, Julia Borgini, Julia Skott, Julie Henderson, Juliette Kelley, Juneta Key, Jyll Chase, Kai Kiser, Karen Frisa, Karin Forno, Kat Sklar, Kate Hagborg, Kate Krake, Katherine Gann, Kathie

Giltinan , Kathleen A Conery, Kathleen Pigeon, Katie Forrest, Katie M, Katie Summers Reid, Katrina Gould, Kay H Neill, Keelia Murphy, Kellie Small, Kelly Griffin, Kelly Lockhart, Kelly Surina, KidLit Craft, Kim Mackenzie, Kim Werker, Kimberley Burkovich, Kimberly Anne, Kimberly Carr, Kirsten Saxton, KJ DellAntonia, Kristin Fischer, Kristin Hilberg, Kristin Strout, Kylo Taylor, LadyPawPaw, Lamar Dickson, Laura Lohner, Lauren Woods, Laurie Anderson, Layla Khoury-Hanold, Lene Andersen, Lily Johnson, Linda McDonald, Linda Moore, Lisa C., Lisa Doherty, Lisa Durso, Liza Laird, Liza Q. Wirtz, Lizz Fransen, Louisa Brooke-Holland, Luisa de Lucca, Lynette Carter, Lynn Houlihan, Maggie Menane, Maile Topliff, Maile Topliff, Malia Jackson, Maria Frazelle , Mariah-Faye, Marie, Marie Hodgkinson, Marie Irshad, Marika Leino, Marla Holt, Marrije Schaake, Martha Dupecher, Martha Neely, Mary E Lasher, Mary Hower, Mary Lynn Sutherland, Mary M Barnett, Mary-Elena Carr, Meagan Smith, Meghan Kroll, Mel Climo, Melanie Weiss, Melena Torretta, Melissa Williams, Meridith Shepherd, Michele M, Michelle Maida, Michelle McQuade Dewhirst, Michelle Toich, Mindy Owen, Miranda Jarnot, Monna McDiarmid, Mya , Nancy K Bowker, Naomi S, Naomi Stenberg, Natalie Luhrs, Natalie Tindall, Neelam Bhojani, Nicolas Lemieux, Noreen Stone, Orna Ross, Patty Sundberg, Paul Worthington, Phyllis Kaelin, Pilar Orti, Polly A Berseth, Portia Carryer, R.L. Merrill , Rachel Brown, Rachel Lightner, Rainaterror , Ray Janikowski, Rebecca Hunter, Rebecca McDonald, Rebecca Robinson, Rebecca Wendt, Rita Szollos, RL Edwards, RL Pryor, Robert E. Stutts, Robin Myers, Robynn Weldon, Ronak Patel, Rosa Quinones, Rose Edvalson, Rosie Radcliffe, Rukma Sen, Ruzanna Gasparyan, Sally Demarest, Sally littlefield, Sam

Rory, Sandi Davis, Sandi Shelton, Sandy Menard, Sandy Miranda, Sara Black, Sara Schley, Sara Watkins, Sarah B., Sarah Barkin, Sarah Mackey, Sarah McCraw Crow, Sarah Sharp, Shalane Shipe, Shannon Harris, Sharon Weiss, Shaun McKinnon, Shenoa Carroll-Bradd, Signe Ross , Skyler Mason, Sophie Berti, Sophie Littlefield, Stacy L Frazer, Stephania Papi, Stephanie Bond, Stephanie Klose, Stephannie Tallent, Stephen Houghton, Sue Bennett, Sue Hunt, Sue Roth, Susan Eiseman Levitin, Susan Smith, Susanna Connaughton, Susanne Dunlap, Suzanne Burns, Tammy Wetzel, Tara East, Tara Swiger, Tavia Smalley, Tawnie Ashley, Teri Simonds, Terrisa Singleton, Tess Enterline, Theresa Rogers, Tina Ambury, Toby Neal, Tom Holbrook, Toni Finley, Tracy Bishop, Trudy MacArtor, Tuomas Makinen, V.E. Griffith, Valerie Ihsan, Vanessa Kier, Veronica Wolff, Vivian T., Wendy Johnson, William Aperance, Zach Bohannon, ZhanTao Yang.

Thank you so much.